JELLY BEAN

versus

DR. JEKYLL & MR. HYDE

---

written
for the SAFETY
of our CHILDREN
and the WELFARE
of our DOGS

by

C.W. MEISTERFELD

Illustrations
by Darlene Perez

M R K Publishing

The Publishing House Truly Dedicated to Man's Best Friend

Library of Congress Catalogue
No. 89-91639

ISBN 0-9601292-5-1

M R K Publishing
448 Seavey
Petaluma, CA 94952
(707) 763-0056

Printed by Patterson Printing, Benton Harbor, Michigan, U.S.A.

WHY YOU SHOULD READ THIS BOOK

Whether you have a new puppy, a "problem dog", or just want to act properly around dogs, you should read this book. It could save your dog's life and, at least equally important, save you, innocent children and friends from the horrors of dog bites and from the nightmare of having to put your dog to sleep.

The good news is that it will teach you how to reach a positive, mutually satisfactory, happy relationship with your dog without using negative methods in his training, such as intimidation, force, punishment, and pain. Even more amazing, it will enable you to do this *because you abstain from these negative methods.* All other books advocate coercion in one form or another, which can lead to problems and even develop a dangerous dog which then must be destroyed.

The truly different methods explained and described in this book are based on over 35 years of experience in the *uniformly successful* training of dogs of all breeds and ages. Even more important, in over 25 years of specializing in the rehabilitation of problem dogs, many dogs were saved from death by these methods and returned to their happy owners as safe and well-mannered pets .

So what's the magic pill? The system of psychological dog training is based on the *unwavering, consistent attention to development of mutual respect and trust between dog and master accomplished with only positive reinforcement.*

The word *unwavering* is the key. Many times harsh discipline, intimidation and physical punishment techniques endorsed by others *seem* to work and are easier and more satisfying, temporarily. However, in the long run they are detrimental to the pet.

Let's take the simple case of a happy puppy who has spent several carefree weeks frolicking outside in the warm summer sun with his affectionate new family. Autumn comes. He is invited indoors and promptly relieves himself on the new white living room rug. The master, who has read the time-honored remedy in training books, promptly grabs the puppy by the scruff of the neck, rubs his nose in the excrement and tosses him out the front door into the cold rain. It works, the dog does not make that mistake again.

Think of the impact if this procedure were used on a young child. The psychiatrists would have a heyday tracing the effect throughout his life. There is no doubt that a few traumatic experiences like this can change your loving puppy into a dangerous dog later in life. In fact, intimidation, force, and physical punishment are the main roots of many of our dog problems today, as case histories prove. In combination with permissiveness, these negative methods can produce schizophrenic dogs with Dr. Jekyll & Mr. Hyde personalities. On the other hand, you can have a happy, reliable, loyal dog of any breed by using the system of psychological training with positive reinforcement advocated here.

How can you avoid the pitfalls and learn to use the positive approach?

We'll explain it in seven steps.

(1) In the first chapter we present the *true and detailed story of a dog* with excellent breeding and experienced, loving owners. In his personal contribution, Dick Flinn explains how his pet (the cover dog) turned into a menace. Paul K. and Barbara Trojan, as family friends, had the opportunity to observe this unfortunate development.

(2) Next, the *different facets of a dog's personality* will be outlined, starting with the *basic concepts of dog behavior,* which will serve as the cornerstone for your understanding. You'll see how and why this dog and millions of others are being forced into disobedience and all kinds of misbehavior, such as barking, chasing, property destruction, biting, and killing.

(3) *Testing and analyzing* of dogs reveals the roots of their specific problems. The exact cause of the cover dog's problem is defined.

(4) *Conditioning and training* set the signals for the behavior of every dog in the right or wrong direction. The faults and errors of established *traditional methods* and their dire consequences for the dogs, their owners, and others are exposed.
The advantages of the *totally positive system of psychological dog training* are put forth.

(5) The undeniable evidence of the need for *mutual respect* in dog training combined with *positive reinforcement* is documented with redemption and successful reprogramming of an otherwise doomed pet, resulting in the metamorphosis of "Doc" to "Jellybean".

With his personal comment, Dick Flinn describes his individual experience during this important process. This is supported by the testimony of the witnesses Paul K. and Barbara Trojan.

(6) In *Fiction and Facts* the prevailing misconceptions and their contribution to many dog problems culminating in severe bites are described.

(7) "The Better Way" highlights *how you can better relate to your pet.*

A collection of case histories is used throughout to illustrate and emphasize the theoretical statements.

The whole thrust of this book is to *help you avoid* many *mistakes* in starting with a new dog and to *give you hope and support* in retraining an old dog with bad habits.

C.W. Meisterfeld
Petaluma, California
April, 1989

Dedicated to Winnie and "Mrs. B.,"
the two individuals who started me on
my journey to discovering the uniqueness
of Man's Best Friend.
To both, Love and Light.

— C.W.M.

ACKNOWLEDGEMENTS

RICHARD A. FLINN

The author of the PROLOGUE and the cover dog's case history is Richard A. Flinn, Professor Emeritus of Materials, Science and Engineering at the University of Michigan, Ann Arbor.

After obtaining his doctorate at M.I.T., he taught for over 35 years at the University, published three books and over a hundred papers, and consulted extensively in Failure Analysis. He and his wife Edwina have also had a lifelong interest in Springer Spaniels. Their dogs have served as pets, guardians of their children, hunting companions for quail, partridge, ducks and geese, and as field trial competitors.

I am especially thankful to Richard and Edwina Flinn for their personal contributions to this book. In their commendable determination to help innocent dogs and their caring owners they did not hesitate to share with the reader the details of their personal involvement in the trials and tribulations experienced with their dog.

HEIDI G. MEISTERFELD

Although God's plans are not always revealed to us we can, through reflection, become aware of the intricate parts we play in them. My gratitude for your part in creating this book goes far beyond my expression of thanks, as every reader will feel. And if dogs could talk they would agree. Thanks.

ERNEST F. PECCI, M.D.

Ernest F. Pecci, M.D., specialist in child psychology, author of "*I love you/I hate you*", is the founder and a governing board member of Rosebridge Graduate School of Integrative Psychology in Walnut Creek, California. Because of the relevance between child rearing methods and dog training techniques, I included some of his significant findings regarding negative and positive conditioning methods in child rearing.

PAUL K. AND BARBARA TROJAN

The witnesses to "Doc's" fall, and "Jellybean's" rise are Paul K. Trojan, Acting Dean of Engineering at the University of Michigan (Dearborn), his wife Barbara, and their daughter Lynn. Springer Spaniels have always been their preferred breed, as pets and for hunting. Barbara Trojan has also been an avid student of horse training methods.

THE EDITOR

Many thanks to Mary Gary for her assistance in editing this book.

THE ILLUSTRATOR

A native of California, Darlene Perez believes in living her life doing things she enjoys the most. A lifelong fascination with animals led her into dog and horse training and made animals preferred objects of her multifaceted artistic talent.

THE TYPESETTER

Thanks and appreciation to Janet Elliott Butcher for the great typesetting job.

THE HARVARD MEDICAL SCHOOL HEALTH LETTER

Thanks for granting us the right to reprint "Dog Bites and Children's Faces," *The Harvard Medical School Health Letter*, 11/1984. Individual subscriptions ($18.00 per year) and bulk subscriptions (reduced rates on 50 or more copies per month) are available. Contact THE HARVARD MEDICAL SCHOOL HEALTH LETTER, 79 Garden St., Cambridge, MA 02138. Telephone (617) 495-5234.

THE PATTERSON PEOPLE

Many thanks for proving your company's concept of the "Three E's." It's Excellent. A special thanks to Linda.

TABLE OF CONTENTS

TABLE OF CONTENTS (con't.)

PROLOGUE

Why should a professor of engineering write a prologue to a book about dog behavior and training and even contribute a personal story?

First of all I have had an absorbing interest in dogs as pets, for hunting, and for field trials for over 40 years. Also, as a good academic, I have made a thorough literature search on dog training and followed all the experts. I thought I knew a great deal about training until last fall, after a series of dramatic incidents with our dog "Doc", a Springer Spaniel.

This experience is the real reason I am writing this prologue and to assure you that the near-tragic case of "Doc/Jellybean", which is woven through the text, is absolutely authentic and could happen to you.

How many people realize that an overdose of affection coupled with traditional negative disciplinary methods can lead to a dangerous dog? Even more significant, how many can accept the fact that it is more important and difficult to train the owners than the dog? The new attitude developed in the owners, as an emotional control, may be as vital as saving the dog.

This book is unique in that C.W. Meisterfeld has designed a system of psychological dog training which *only* uses positive reinforcement and is based on the genuine understanding of the dog's nature. Other books contain a good deal of helpful material but have the fatal flaw that negative and painful methods are advocated as well. This weak link leads to failure and tragedy.

In a positive vein you are shown how, by giving up the self-gratification of excessive affection and permissiveness on one hand and the release of anger on the other, you can develop a lasting, natural, enjoyable relationship with your dog.

All this we have personally experienced. Let me tell you our personal story as the first chapter of C.W. Meisterfeld's valuable book on dogs.

Richard A. Flinn
Ann Arbor, Michigan

CHAPTER I

A COMMON CASE HISTORY

Excellent Dog + Negative Training Methods
+ Permissiveness
= Disaster

By Dick Flinn

Michigan is a wonderful state but even the natives admit it is a mite cold in winter. So finally, in January 1986, we were on our way to our winter retreat in northern California, near the shores of the Pacific. Marvelling at the deep green hills and the beautiful surroundings, we passed a professional billboard in the town of Petaluma which caught our attention:

> PETALUMA'S
> CANINE PSYCHOANALYST
> • THERAPIST
> • TRAINER
> C.W. MEISTERFELD
> Tel. 763-0056

We leaned back and roared in laughter. These Californians will buy anything!

My wife Edwina and I both love dogs very much. We have had dogs for over 40 years. We reflected on several litters of Springer Spaniels we had raised, the dogs we had campaigned at national field trials, and wondered what was wrong with people out here that they would need of all things, a *dog psychoanalyst!* However, we did admit to ourselves that maybe our old dog "Doc", who had died some time ago, could have been under better control. At many a trial after getting out about 40 yards he would become whistle-deaf and flush birds out of gun range. But everyone said he was just hardheaded with too much show stock in his background.

13

After getting settled in California, we decided to get back into field trials. An avid field trial buff and good friend in Michigan had just imported and bred a pair of dogs from England with solid, impeccable, field trial championship lines. He offered us the pick of the litter. We flew to Michigan and took our time to study the antics of the wonderful, frisky puppies. Almost every time our attention was attracted by a certain dog, who was lively and dominant and always did something remarkable. For example, he would grab a large branch and tow two or three litter mates. Also, he was very trusting and never hesitated to approach us. This was obviously "our dog" and we called him "Doc" after our old campaigner.

We brought him home at just the right time—seven weeks old. He not only travelled perfectly in the car and never whined, but also took the trip without problems when we flew from Michigan back to California.

He was the friendliest and most curious puppy we could imagine, playful and very, very intelligent. You almost had to outthink him. He was interested in everything that was going on around him and it was often difficult to stop his urge to explore his immediate environment and the world.

He became easily housebroken by using the method of rubbing his nose in an unwanted deposit and tossing him outside. He seemed at first a little shocked and angry at this but learned fast and never after made the same mistake. He understood the basic commands rapidly—hup (sit), heel, stay, here. But one small problem developed. While he learned these commands readily, he did not always want to comply. We could almost see him think, "Should I or shouldn't I obey?" Altogether, his learning progress was remarkable, and his memory was phenomenal.

As all puppies do, he loved to play rough and chew on things. Shoes and socks were his favorite objects. We played chew-biting with him, and he pulled everything within his reach into his crate. Also, we bought him raw beef bones to satisfy his chewing needs. Unfortunately, this did not curb his appetite for our things, such as shoes or sweaters, which were beyond recovery when we found them.

All in all, we had a happy time with him and thought that if he could be treated like a member of the family even to sitting in the chairs, romping through the house playfully with a sock or shoe of his choice, he would be a better dog. However, we wondered a little about one of his favorite sports—biting our wrist or ankle but never breaking the skin.

When he was about four months old, Edwina caught Doc with one of my shoes. She yelled at him and tried to wrestle the shoe out of his locked jaws. He dropped it, but snatched her hand instead slightly breaking the skin.

When Edwina told me about this incident, I became really concerned, but then I dismissed it as nothing serious, just the usual puppy behavior, which will vanish with his growing maturity...

As Doc grew older, his romps through the house became more spirited. He loved to jump on beds. This was quite different from our former dogs who were kept in kennels and only allowed in the house as a rare privilege. But we thought we were developing a closer rapport which would help us later with control in the trials.

When we surprised little Doc in wrongdoing, we punished him with a slap, and yelled "No", as recommended in the numerous books we had acquired over the years. Despite Doc's extraordinary intelligence and memory, all the slapping and hitting did not seem to have the desired effect.

At about six months, because of his rapid learning progress, we decided to start training for retrieving. I had always used the "force" method with my dogs, which starts with squeezing the dog's paw to get him to open his mouth to receive the dummy. Doc growled at this, and I substituted a method of pressing his lips against his teeth. Doc did not like this either, but after a few sessions was holding the dummy, although grudgingly.

Then came the preparation for the field trials. He was retrieving well. He was given free rein to run on 11 acres of cover rich in quail, rabbit, and deer scent. In following the best published advice he became the fastest, birdiest puppy we had ever seen. He had been carefully introduced to shot, and we were resolved to steady him for the first spring trial. He was placed on a loose rope attached to a stake and told to stay. Then we tossed fluttering wing-plucked pigeons by him. If he broke he would get flipped by the rope. He became perfectly steady when on the rope but when he was allowed to hunt freely in the field, he continued to break on flushing birds. We partially cured this by chasing him, grabbing him by the ears, blowing the whistle in his ears and returning him to the place where he broke, slamming him down unceremoniously. We remember well how he looked at us in amazement during this discipline and then started to growl.

Soon afterwards, I introduced Doc to his first game while quail hunting in Virginia. Doc did not show any gun-shyness and performed perfectly. I returned very happily from this hunting trip and was extremely proud of him.

The first official field trial for Doc was scheduled for February, 1988. Now it was up to Doc, seven months old, to prove what he had learned so far. I was very excited and optimistic about the results. Doc quartered well, drove into his first bird, hupped, and waited for command to retrieve. Then he started back gaily with a fine hold on the bird, but to my amazement stopped and sat almost 20 yards away still holding the bird. He would not come further. So I walked calmly over to him and had to use the force method of pressing his lips on his teeth to extricate the bird. He responded with a very deep growl. I snapped on his leash and withdrew quietly.

When we got home I attached a long light cord to his collar and gave the end to my wife. Then I put out a bird for retrieve within the range of the cord and sent Doc. He stopped halfway back under the shade of a tree. Promptly I gave the "come-in" signal and Edwina yanked gently. He got the point and never stopped again.

Between February and September (7 to 13 months) I had a chance to get Doc really ready. He loved to make long water retrieves on Gull Lake in the summer. In the field he was quartering fairly well except when deer scent attracted him. Then he would be gone for a half hour, coming back only when he was exhausted and covered with mud. He was clearly in charge of his conduct in the field. When he was retrieving, he would mark at long distances. The only trouble was that he would also mark a bracemate's birds and often break to get them too. We gave him extensive ear-yanking following the traditional method.

Finally, he seemed ready for the fall circuit I had always dreamed of, starting in Maine in September, the Midwest in October and finishing in the California mountains in November. I entered him in puppy and amateur all-age stakes across the country. Fortunately, in the Maine Open in the First Series, he got the strong scent of a runner, took it all the way out in a marsh—away from the other course—and got a spectacular flush and retrieve. For his second bird he quickly made game and retrieved well to be called back. Here we began on a rise of ground, and he could see the other dog and guns working the marsh on the other course. He stopped and watched instead of quartering. He paid no attention to any signals or commands. He just stood there like a *general* overlooking the battlefield ahead. Then he remembered that there were birds in the marsh and took off to the other course.

I had to suffer and watch this independent behavior even in puppy stakes where dogs were run alone. After a few casts he would scent a bird perhaps 20 yards away. (These stakes are always run upwind.) He would cock his head and decide upon the route of approach and how fast to move. Of course, any hesitancy is often labeled blinking or bird shyness, but this was not the case. He was figuring out how to catch the bird! Then, after flushing and sitting steady, he developed another independent trait. The procedure is for the judge to tell the handler to send his dog. Doc "read the judge's lips" and I would hear over and over again: "He went a mite early, didn't he." I told the judge it was ESP but it did not sell very well...

The results of the tour were a host of good new friends, quite a lot of good advice in traditional methods, and newer ones involving shock collars. "A great many professionals use them!" As for ribbons, Doc got fourth place in a field of four in the last puppy trial of the season. What a kind judge! Although steady, Doc gave his usual stop and go, "I am in charge" type of performance, and did leave "a mite early" on retrieves.

Now came the sad part of Doc's career. It was a continuation of a series of increasingly negative and serious incidents. The older he grew, the more belligerently he reacted. Doc became more and more possessive and always needed to get something in exchange when we wanted to take something away from him.

He had been living in a crate in the station wagon a large share of the time. Now he did not like being confined in a kennel or crate. Although he would still jump over the tailgate into the crate on command, he would growl and bare his teeth as I locked the door. Every time when I went up to his run to get him for training he would run back into his house and just roll one big questioning eye at me.

17

I would open the gate, move away, and *only then would he come.* I also remember one other bad reaction. He would tug unmercifully on his leash during our daily walks until I picked up a switch. Then he would cower and retreat so skillfully on the leash that I rarely could give him an authoritative whack.

Now back to his behavior at a year and a half. In addition to the growling upon kenneling, my wife Edwina had a shattering experience. She was in the back of our son's house (a confined space) with Doc, whose nylon collar had come off. As she tried to put his collar back on, Doc suddenly lunged at her and almost knocked her down. He pulled the sweater off her left shoulder and went for her throat. He would have seriously injured her if the large house dog, which fortunately was in the same yard and close by, had not interfered and rescued her, allowing her to reach the door and safety. She was very frightened and shaken up.

When I heard Edwina's cries I rushed to the yard and took Doc out to the car. He looked bewildered and sorry and wanted to be friendly. I had him sit behind the tailgate. However, when I ordered him to jump into his crate he refused. I started to thump him. Suddenly he lunged at me, aiming at my throat and tearing my sweater. Somehow I got him in tow and attached an electronic collar which I had just bought. After getting him in his crate and locking the door he growled menacingly. That's when I shocked him for the first time. However, the shock collar did not seem to have any curbing effect on his aggressiveness; it made it even worse. Doc continued to growl in his crate and showed no remorse.

A few weeks later Edwina was removing ticks from Doc's body and experienced another assault. When she worked on his inner thigh to look for ticks, all of a sudden Doc changed personalities. His eyes narrowed and he jumped up on her, ready to bite. She was in a corner of the kitchen and alone, scared to death. She yelled "hup" (sit) and stuck out her leg to keep him away from her body. She cried for help. Fortunately, I was in the next room and hearing her screams, immediately came to her rescue. The dog was still glaring at her when I snatched him and took him outside.

The day after this event, Doc was again loving and sweet. We were at a loss to understand how this dog could change personalities so suddenly and frequently, from an obedient, faithful comrade and friend, into an unreliable, rebellious, dangerous adversary. We really became concerned that Doc might hurt us or others seriously, especially children. We could not trust him anymore. He had too often exhibited a split personality, a Dr. Jekyll and Mr. Hyde. We telephoned friends across the country for advice. The top veterinary authorities, after hearing about the case, said there was no hope due to an apparent "genetic failure." Their recommendation was to destroy Doc.

When we realized that we had to give Doc up, who had been with us for a year and a half, we really were desperate. Despite his escapades and disturbed personality, we loved him and felt close to him. We did not want to accept this fate for our great friend.

As a final gesture we turned to our local veterinarian to have Doc castrated. The vet did not think that neutering would change Doc's aggression. He suggested instead a conference with guess who—the dog psychoanalyst in Petaluma we had laughed at, who had successfully reprogrammed numerous dogs with the most serious problems, such as destructiveness, biting and viciousness, etc.

That's how we met C.W. (Bill) Meisterfeld, to whom we entrusted Doc for reprogramming. We were overjoyed that there was a chance to save Doc's life and return him as a friendly, sociable and safe companion.

Witnesses I

by Paul and Barbara Trojan

We have trained Springer Spaniels for over 30 years with our friends, Dick and Edwina. Naturally, we have known Doc from his earliest days when Dick brought him by our home just after he had picked him up from the kennel. Even at seven weeks he showed all the right traits—boundless energy, but directed to following scents, or tugging and hauling, or just playing with anyone who would pay attention to him. Even then he seemed to be quite intelligent, almost thinking out any move before dashing in one direction or another.

We remember when he was only five months old how precocious he was at retrieving. Despite the large tailgate crowd on the golf course at the Michigan-Michigan State Game, Dick could plant a dummy a hundred yards away and Doc would retrieve it on command, ignoring the whistles of the crowd.

All through the year Doc seemed to be improving in ability and intelligence but, perhaps because of living very closely with Dick and Edwina, he was not under good control. He needed to be kept on leash or he would go for miles if given his freedom in a yard.

A year later at the same game he showed phenomenal retrieving of multiple dummies at great distance, but there was a disquieting circumstance. When he was locked up in his crate in the back of the station wagon he would growl fiercely and bare his teeth at passers-by and even at Dick when he put him back in his crate. Also, in walking him around on a leash, he would invariably tug as though he were the boss. However, we hoped Doc would overcome this aggressiveness and his independent behavior.

When we learned that Doc had attacked Edwina and Dick, we became very concerned. We agreed with Dick that something had to be done, and quickly. We had several top-drawer friends in university veterinary schools whom we could consult about this case. They were unanimously of the opinion that Doc should be put away. We did not have the heart to tell Dick directly and gave him the names of several of the experts. He contacted them and got the bad news firsthand. However, he told us that he did not intend to give up so easily. Then we heard from him that he was going to see Bill Meisterfeld as a last resort. We really wished that there was hope for Doc.

CHAPTER II

DIFFERENT FACETS OF A DOG'S PERSONALITY

Basic Concepts of Dog Behavior

Now that we have heard Doc's story from his owner's point of view let us build up a background of basic concepts before we probe further into this case. These are needed not only to analyze Doc's problem which is not just typical of Springer Spaniels. The same disturbed behavior can occur in any dog, pure or mixed breed, from toy types, to Old English Sheep dogs, to mutts. Therefore, it is very important to understand the different facets of a dog's personality and behavior—how and why he responds in a certain way in a given situation. Also, this comprehension is the precondition for the proper training and control of any dog.

Whether we are speaking of the 18-month-old Doc or a 10-year-old German Shepherd, every dog's behavior is the product of his heredity (genes) and his environment. Let us discuss these factors so you can make an assessment for *your dog.*

1. **Inherited or Genetic Behavior**
   a) Original genetic behavior
   b) Modified genetic behavior through selective breeding by man
2. **Random Behavior Self-Acquired by the Dog**, based on
   a) the dog's survival and other instincts
   b) the dog's self-gratification
   c) the dog's ability to imitate
3. **Proper Behavior as a Result of Training by the Owner** (and specific behavior due to special training, such as in case of dogs for the disabled, etc.), based on
   a) the dog's original genetic behavior
   b) the dog's modified breed-standard behavior

1. **Inherited or Genetic Behavior**

    a) **Original genetic behavior** developed due to the need to survive. The strong instincts to chase and hunt, to run in packs, to dominate a weaker animal, and to use the teeth for self-defense and attack, were imprinted in our dogs long before recorded time and are still present today. The ability to mimic behavior has been an asset in the dogs' learning process.

    b) **Genetic behavior was modified** by crossing certain breeds of dogs in order to enhance particular or reduce unwanted behavioral traits and instincts. Selective breeding is also practiced today for this purpose to adjust the dog to man's specific needs. Alert watch dogs, like the Lhasa Apso and Shih Tzu, are bred to warn the owners of trespassing intruders. Herding dogs are bred for guarding and herding our livestock. Hunting dogs, such as German Shorthair Pointers, are intended to hunt both feather (birds) and furred animals, Labradors to retrieve game, and fighting dogs, like the Chindo and Pitbull, to fight for the master and also to protect him and his property. Generally speaking, with this modification of genetic behavior, man developed the unique attribute of the dog—to be highly trainable, coupled with his innate drive to serve him.

    Egyptians applied this understanding thousands of years ago. The walls of ancient Egyptian Pharaohs' tombs show various breeds of dogs (some of which are recognized today in the AKC breed standards). These portray dogs hunting for man, protecting his family, and as pets lying at the feet of the master.

2. **Random Self-Acquired Behavior**

    When a dog is *not trained*, he develops *random self-acquired behavior* based on his genetic makeup, involving his survival and other instincts, and the ability to imitate behavior.

    From the moment they are born the behavior of young puppies is shaped by their mother. They learn to cope with their environment by imitating her actions and responses. If the mother has behavior problems she will transfer them to her pups if they stay with her too long. In this way a puppy can also learn aggressiveness toward other dogs or animals which are usually immune from attack.

    To illustrate this important point let us consider a case history.

Clients of mine had an aggressive male Golden Retriever who was left untrained. Before they came to me for consultation and evaluation of their dog—to find out if he could be saved—they followed the advice of a training book, "Your dog needs companionship. Get another dog of the opposite sex, and this will solve the problem." So they acquired a female dog. The result was that, after a short time, the bitch mimicked the male and became aggressive as well.

For a dual problem of this nature their book contained a simple solution: Puppies could certainly calm down aggressive dogs.

So they placed their hope in breeding the dogs. From the litter of five they kept a male puppy. He was brought up by his parents and did not receive any additional training from the owners.

When the puppy was about nine months of age, a three-month-old puppy of the neighbors came into their yard to play with the dog family.

In times past, there was a strict genetic behavior code among dogs that under no circumstances would bitches or puppies be harmed. However, this behavior pattern of respect does not seem to exist anymore in the present genetic memory bank of many dogs. These three dogs proved this point in a shocking way.

As soon as the little puppy approached the dog family, it was immediately attacked by all three dogs and practically torn apart.

This case shows that the unfortunate combination of three facts led to disaster:

1) The oldest dog was not trained nor were the bitch and puppy.
2) The bitch and the puppy mimicked the aggressive behavior of the male dog who was the pack leader.
3) The behavior of respect for young puppies had been weakened because the dogs were not trained.

Random self-learned behavior is accidental, unstructured, and unreliable and in most cases not acceptable or tolerable in terms of our social standards. It only serves the self-gratification of the dog. Therefore, it is quite natural that an *untrained* herding dog instinctively will try to herd the house cat and chase the livestock to the point of exhaustion. This can even lead to the weird result of the death of cows or premature abortion of their calves. An *untrained* hunting dog will hunt 24 hours a day just for himself. An *untrained* guard dog will instinctively attack and bite any stranger or intruder violating his territory.

3. Proper Behavior as a Result of Training

Despite his hereditary nature to serve, a dog can only fit into the specific lifestyles of human environment if he is especially trained for this purpose.

In the chapters ahead we shall see how the desired behavior as the goal of the training process can be reinforced and promoted with negative or positive stimuli. However, the best guarantee for the successful adaptation of a dog to his special environment is his conditioning or training with *positive* techniques, i.e., psychological methods based on mutual respect. Only with positive reinforcement and occasional rewards can the desired, reliable behavior be attained without any lapses on a long-term basis. Also, positive reinforcement is a more reliable motivator because it is not mentally stressful.

SUMMARY

1. The behavior of any dog can always be modified by environmental influences.
2. Certain instincts and behavior traits can be intensified or reduced in a breed through specific selection by the breeder.
3. If the dog is not trained, the genetic instincts will run wild leading to perversion such as chasing in a pack to molest and kill sheep and livestock.
4. Appropriate training will contribute to the development of a well-balanced dog who is well-adjusted to human conditions.
5. Training a dog will also enhance his behavior for which his breed is noted, e.g., herding, hunting, retrieving, fighting. Then, he will not practice it for self-gratification, but only on command for his owner.

Instincts and the Law of Survival

Instincts in man have become dulled in the course of evolutionary development giving way to rational thinking. However, children growing up under circumstances where primitive instincts prevail and education is lacking, adjust to their environment accordingly. Their instincts will be strongly involved, to the detriment of their rational thinking ability, leading to automatic primitive reactions in response to their immediate environmental stimuli. After maturity, they will transfer this way of interrelating to other, different environments. Generally speaking, the quality and quantity of our initial, early conditioning usually dominates and controls our later patterns of behavior.

The law of survival governs the existence of all living beings. Only those individuals of a species which are the strongest and fittest in coping with the existing environmental conditions ensure the further existence of their kind. When environmental conditions become detrimental to the existence of a certain species and not enough individuals are able to adjust and adapt, this species is doomed and will die out—a process of natural selection. The survival instinct is the strongest of all instincts in all animals. For them it is a necessity and works as a protection mechanism against harm.

Our domestic dogs are, as animals, still very closely connected to and dependent on Mother Nature's fundamental laws; and their instincts are more intense than ours. Thus, the survival instinct of a dog will be triggered by any action perceived by him as a threat or attack, and lead to an automatic, unconditioned response—flight or fight. The level of the dog's assertiveness and the specific circumstances will determine the choice. In general, the dog will prefer the flight reaction. Only if he sees no chance for flight will he fight and use his teeth.

Each time we create a threatening situation for the dog, we condition and strengthen his survival instinct, translated into his flight or fight mechanism, which is influenced by his mental and physical strength.

For this reason, forceful, painful training methods very often create fear or aggressive biters, who can perceive even new, non-hazardous situations as threatening due to fear conditioning.

The same holds true for completely untrained dogs who rely only on inherited primitive instincts, of which the survival is the predominant one.

SUMMARY

1. The reason for a dog's aggressiveness can be fear when his survival instinct is triggered.
2. Survival behavior is the dog's only choice if he is untrained or trained with threatening methods.

The Ranking or Pecking Order

Being a pack animal, the dog's social interaction with other dogs, other animals, and people is based on the ranking order system, also called "pecking order," in which individuals have to know their place and role in the overall structure, and the whole group follows a leader. Thanks to Mother Nature's creativity and versatility the dog, as an animal from another evolutionary level, has become closely involved with mankind due to the similarity of his social needs and his adaptability and usefulness. Originally, in exchange for work and service, the dog received food and shelter. Man, as the provider, was the recognized superior in this established system. Nowadays, dogs are largely deprived of their original task—to work for us. There are hunting dogs who have never smelled a pheasant or rabbit, herding dogs who never had a glimpse of livestock. Instead, they have become predominantly social companions—pets. This is a very important role too, but contributes to their increasing dependency.

A dog perceives his human family as his pack, and wants his owner to be the respected authority in the top position. Every dog in a human family has the innate need to follow a human leader as a result of his pack instinct. For this reason, it is an unhealthy relationship when a dog is treated as an equal. A dog cannot be equal due to the limits of his genetic background and complete dependency on his owner.

The owner should always be aware that the dog's inferior position in this setting has nothing to do with suppression, disrespect or exploitation. It is the consequence of an evolutionary process, as well as a typical behavior pattern of the dog — a completely natural configuration.

Unfortunately, in some man/dog relationships, dogs are not only treated as equals, but as superiors. When an owner does not exercise his head position and responsibility, a strong-willed dog is forced to take over by reason of his "pack/status" instinct. Somebody has to be in charge, and that individual is entitled to express likes and dislikes and to *enforce* them. The predominant behavior of a highly assertive, strong-willed dog will be demanding and aggressive and his owner has to give in to the challenges and cater to the dog. However, neither the dog nor the owner can be happy in a role contradictory to the laws of nature.

Such a dog becomes more and more frustrated and angry, and when a certain level is reached, needs release and explodes at an object serving as the outlet. Sometimes, the dog will first focus on things, and then proceed to living beings, such as other dogs, other animals, and people (especially children) and turn on them without warning. One day the dog, having spared his owner so far from physical harm, will attack him without the owner deviating from his ordinary routine. The mental overload and adrenal overcharge are responsible.

A dog with a low assertiveness (will-to-power), who is not able to handle the leader role, becomes emotionally disturbed and more susceptible to physical illnesses. He can show his frustration and dissatisfaction in destructive and annoying behavior, bark excessively, soil the house, run away, etc., and eventually bite as well.

The dog is put into a position he does not want, and negative consequences develop. He is being deprived of what he really needs— a firm structure with man as the master in the center—and the possibility of serving and pleasing him on request on a daily basis, complimented with a little praise and affection for good performance.

Have you ever watched how happy a dog is when he can retrieve a ball or a stick for his master and receives praise for his work? This is truly dog heaven. In comparison, observe the reaction of an idle, spoiled dog when he has to vacate his comfortable place on the couch to a visitor or even his owner.

Nobody can expect a dog to respect a person who permanently caters to him and even treats the dog better than a human being without requesting anything in terms of training or service. The dog feels in a power position and will always manifest his own demands which the owner has to meet because he has become the subordinate.

A dog is only able to understand simple facts when interrelating with his owner in daily life. Are you behaving as my master or do you permit me to be *your* boss? For a dog it is as easy as that. He cannot comprehend our ideological concepts and motives for human relationships with equality as a predominant component.

A dog does not have our sense of freedom, either. According to our understanding, we assume we are depriving the dog of a paramount natural right if we don't let him run freely and roam for his pleasure. We forget that animals living in the wild never run without reason. They do it for survival.

It is detrimental for a pet to be permitted to run uncontrolled. This conditions his primitive instincts and promotes disobedient behavior. In addition, it is irresponsible toward society because of the possible harm to people, livestock, the dog himself, and other animals. Roaming dogs often cause accidents, bite people, contribute to the canine overpopulation, spread diseases, and pollute the environment.

The following case history describes how a dog owner became enlightened about her role in the pecking order.

Chicken Number Two

The caller was concise and direct: "I have a fighting, happy German shepherd. He loves all two-legged creatures. He adores not only adults but also babies and children. But he seems to have a hate-passion for any four-legged animals, dogs and cats especially. When they are around he changes into a ferocious Genghis Khan. Can you do something with him?" Then there was heavy silence which was unusual. Normally, most first phone contacts are pure monologues until the dog owner has expressed the whole history from the purchase of the six-week-old pup, along with blood lines, to the present day problems.

"Yes, lady, I have reprogrammed fighters into lovers. Only it sounds as though for the moment you have both. Maybe your dog does not understand what you desire. Have you spent any time training him to develop communication?"

"That is the reason I am calling you. I was kicked out of an obedience class that I started with two months ago. The trainer told me not to come anymore, until I could control Lollypop's aggressiveness toward other dogs. Lollypop is obedient and works beautifully at home. He knows all the commands, yet once he sees another dog he seems to have a lapse of memory and does not respond at all."

"Didn't the group trainer give you personal instructions?"

"Sure, he told me my dog needed socialization which I would get in the group. And Lollypop enjoyed it. He just could not wait to get into the building after the second week. As the class progressed so did he. Every time a few more of his Genghis Khan genes surfaced. It became so bad that the trainer had me train him on the side of the group. This worked out fine. Only I had to wait upon arrival until everybody was in. The same procedure had to be observed on departure. We could only leave the building after all the owners with their dogs were gone. Meeting someone at the door with his dog would have lead to a major disaster, inevitably ringing the bell in Lollypop's head starting round one. How soon may I see you?"

"Today, if you wish. You could come at 1:00 p.m."

"Great, see you soon."

Right on the button of 1:00 p.m. I watched the car drive in the parking lot. All I could see was a German Shepherd sitting in the passenger seat. His overall appearance dominated the whole front windshield, and I almost took him for the driver. Finally, I could recognize a little lady hugging the steering wheel, squeezed in and glued to the inside of the driver's door. Lollypop commanded three quarters of the total width and half of the bucket seat of his mistress.

Approaching the car, I signaled to the lady to get out of the car and bring the dog to me.

Right after Mrs. Pinch touched the knob of the car door, Lollypop had his feet dug into the parking lot gravel and was pulling her out of the car, tugging her on the leash, dragging her right into the direction of the kennel door, as if he knew why he was here and where he had to go. Lollypop did not even bother to sniff me on passing.

Almost breathless from the efforts to resist Lolly's wild drive and to lead him into my direction, Mrs. Pinch tried to turn Lollypop over to me but her legs were hopelessly entangled in the leash. She only succeeded in her unraveling attempts, after Lollypop had finished his third circle. I caught the leash before his fourth round.

"Oh yes, this is another habit I have not been able to break. Of course, he is just excited but it does get a little exasperating at times."

Lolly proved to me that he was friendly to people by jumping all over me and trying to give me a licky kiss.

"Does he behave like this all the time?"

"Only when I take him somewhere new. He is so curious and wants to check out everybody and everything."

Lollypop had given quite a demonstration of his position in life. The question was, "Could he be reprogrammed, and was it feasible for the owner to do it?" Some six-year-old dogs can be pretty set in their ways.

29

I put him through the tests along with direct contact with other dogs. Yes, he was salvageable from my point of view, but a lot would depend on my consultation with his owner.

The cloud of concern lifted from Mrs. Pinch's face, when I told her that Lollypop's problem would be easy to lick.

"First, permit me to tell you a story that is somewhat similar to yours. I had a Doberman brought to me for training. Blitz's behavior problems were not much different from Lollypop's, but his owner did not get booted out of the group obedience class. As a matter of fact, I was quite surprised when I learned that Blitz took first place out of 73 dogs. Yet his owner did not have any control over him outside of the training school. The problem was that Blitz was trained to follow class training patterns mechanically. The owner never did develop his master/dog relationship. When the dog wanted to do something, such as chase bicyclers down the street, he would not respond to his owner's commands. In other words, Blitz would do as he pleased when something better presented itself. He was top dog.

"Lollypop and you have the same problem. You are Number-Two Chicken in the pecking order, trying to control Number-One Chicken. You need to have a complete reversal of roles and the relationship as a whole, by placing yourself at all times as authority in the top position."

"This sounds easy for you, Mr. Meisterfeld; but after all these years, what chance do I have to change the situation?"

"You have an exceptionally good one. Lollypop carries the key to your desire and it is the most important means in reprogramming a dog's behavioral problems. It is his desire to please and serve you based on mutual respect."

"That's difficult to believe after all the trials and tribulations I have been through with him. Did you let him get near any other dogs?"

"Yes, though he did not seem to comprehend fully, Lollypop respected my command to leave them alone. I walked him down the aisle within one foot of the other dogs' runs, and the second time past he would not even look at them, let alone challenge them, even when a couple of macho dogs challenged him."

"But isn't it normal for a dog to protect his territory and challenge any intruders?"

"Right, but only when he is placed in charge. When the owner is present, he should be in charge. Thus the dog waits for his master to make the decision or first move and to tell him what to do."

"Now I understand and see my mistake. I made too many allowances. Thank you, Mr. Meisterfeld, you helped me very much."

With that, and a copy of *"Hows and Whys of Psychological Dog Training"* in her hand, Mrs. Pinch headed for the kennel exit and Lollypop proceeded to take over and pull her through the door.

I managed to say, "Be sure to use the book," at which she gave Lollypop a whack on the nose with it. He literally flew back to the left side and heeled properly all the way back to the car.

Now that was not what I meant by "use the book." But for the moment it was very effective. And I am sure, once she reads it, Lollypop will be Number-Two Chicken!

SUMMARY
1. There is a natural order in the animal kingdom to follow a leader who is number one.
2. It is natural and necessary to train your dog so that he knows and accepts his proper position in the human family.
3. Your dog should be considered the last number in the pecking order with all human members above.
4. Catering and treating your dog as an equal forces him *to take over and rule you!*

Dominance and Will-to-Power

Some species, like canines, exhibit dominant behavior as a means of establishing leadership and order within their rank and file. This contributes to the survival of the fittest. It is the survival instinct that widely influences the extent of an individual's drive and potential to demonstrate dominance and authority toward his own kind, other animals, and people.

The dominance potential or assertiveness of an animal is expressed in his will-to-power, a genetic behavior trait. Rams, deer and elk fight with their horns and antlers in order to find out who is superior. Canines use their teeth to determine who is the strongest and most dominant in this contest of wills. Thus, the wolf pack leader controls the behavior of his pack very effectively and keeps them in line by expressing his will-to-power with his teeth.

Our domestic dogs also have this inherited behavior pattern to

31

employ their teeth, not only to protect themselves and their offspring or their owners property, but also to demonstrate their will-to-power toward their own kind, other animals, and even people, in order to determine who will dominate.

Even in playfully aggressive encounters, adult dogs express their superiority with their teeth. Usually they will not seriously harm each other if the weaker dog immediately exhibits submissive behavior.

The same applies to little puppies in a litter who are already practicing this aggressive behavior from an early stage showing differences in their assertiveness, i.e., will-to-power, due to their individual personalities.

The individual personalities in dogs encompass a great variety of temperament and character shades which are present and obvious from birth on. There is always one active, willful puppy who is the first to nurse, and another passive and timid one who is the last.

The will-to-power, a fundamental hereditary behavior trait of every dog, grows with maturity and is quite variable. The individual level of the will-to-power is directly related to the physical and mental strength of a dog.

The graph on Page 84 illustrates the typical development pattern of the will-to-power. The vertical scale shows the extent of the will-to-power from its lowest level 1 to the highest level 10. The horizontal scale indicates the age of the dog in months.

In general until the age of about three months the will-to-power remains fairly constant. Then the learning ability begins to accelerate, accompanied by remarkable psychological growth and changes which decisively influence the future behavior of the dog.

The will-to-power gradually increases from three to six months and grows rapidly between six and nine months. It continues to increase from nine to twelve months and then more slowly into maturity. Small breeds are considered mature at 24 months, and large breeds at 36 months. After maturity, the will-to-power remains relatively stable.

Taking the time element of the will-to-power development into consideration, it becomes obvious why behavior problems, especially biting, can frequently be observed in dogs of the age group seven to twelve months. This is the period when they become increasingly assertive and try to establish dominance in their environment. As a natural, inherited behavior trait, they use their teeth for this purpose.

The Teachings of Dolly — or I Am The Boss

Dolly was one of the toy group, a great dog from the start. Though she was small in size, she made up for it in determination and persistence. It was their first dog, and the owners were well informed as to her feeding and care. Her state of health was excellent. As long as they catered to her, everything else was fine too. The only disharmony now and then was created when Dolly did not get her way.

The owners had to discover very early that Dolly did not want to be bothered while eating, which later developed to the point of heavy growling and occasional snapping when somebody had the nerve to intrude on her privacy.

They next learned that Dolly did not like to be left totally alone. In fact, she was like the proverbial infant still tied to the apron strings of her mother. Even when one of her owners went to the bathroom, she would follow, watching what was going on. Of course, when locked out, she would not hesitate to scratch on the door. Rather than risking a hole in the bathroom door, they submitted to letting her be a spectator to all events coming and going. Whenever they tried to leave their apartment without Dolly, she would express her rightful protest to this cruel abandonment with a barking fit. Such behavior could hardly go unnoticed, especially living in an apartment building. The neighbors were understanding and sympathetic at first, but soon a wave of complaints began flooding the manager's office.

The owners conceded that something definitely had to be done. Move? But they liked the view of the Bay and Golden Gate and the rent was also affordable. No, they wouldn't move. But how to keep Dolly from acting up every time they left? The answer was so simple, really. One of them would just have to stay home with Dolly as a companion.

Now this was great for Dolly. However, the couple's social life, their togetherness as husband and wife, was greatly curtailed. As happy as Dolly was with this arrangement, it became clear that it was not the perfect solution.

Then one day some very useful advice was offered. Get a dog sitter. Well, this worked out beautifully for everybody involved. All the sitter had to do was "be there." Dolly thrived and was completely satisfied as long as there was a human being with her. It did not matter who was present, or even if she was petted or not. As long as her "body guard" was on duty, she was peaceful and quiet. Needless to say, her owners were delighted to be able to go out together again. Their marriage improved remarkably.

Unfortunately, there was not always a dog sitter available when needed. That's how they found out that their victory was short-lived and not quite complete. During the day, when the wife did the shopping, Dolly insisted on accompanying her. Dolly simply loved car rides to the shopping centers and would not miss an opportunity for that. It did not even take great effort to convince her mistress of the necessity for taking her along; her howling created a fuss which was compelling enough.

Very soon the wife discovered that she could not shop forever, but was only allotted 20 minutes. She was promptly notified when she was overdue by Dolly's vocal complaints. More than once members of Dolly's audience gathered around the car and reminded her mistress with threatening fists of her neglect of duty toward the poor, lonely and abandoned pet.

When their food stock was very depleted and made it necessary for both of them to go shopping, the owners had to make some more adjustments. First, they would check out the number of people in the supermarket before they even started their shopping spree. When the crowd was small, there was no hesitation. By shopping as a team and using some fast footwork, they managed to get their shopping done in the allotted time. The husband purchased the meat, dairy products, and fruit, while his wife purchased all the other items. Going to separate checkout counters, they reunited with Dolly in the car in less than 20 minutes.

One summer day they took a long weekend trip to Lake Tahoe. Stopping at one of the restaurants, they overstayed the time allowance that Dolly had set. In her frustration, Dolly decided to rearrange and redecorate the interior of the car. She started with chewing the armrests, proceeding to the seats, headrests and carpets. Eight hundred dollars worth of damage in all. After that episode, the next time the owners were a little smarter and more considerate. When they stopped to eat, it was done in shifts. First, one would go in to eat while the other stayed with Dolly. Then vice versa.

However, Dolly became more and more dissatisfied and frustrated with her uncaring owners. She made them face their lack of attention and consideration when she had an opportunity. Once she was locked in the master bedroom when she became a nuisance to some guests. Without hesitation, she systematically tackled seven pairs of shoes and destroyed one shoe of each pair to confront her folks with their injustice and cruelty. But her versatile, ingenious owners found a quick remedy by tranquilizing Dolly the next time when they had guests. If the gathering was small, one pill was considered sufficient. If it was large, they gave Dolly two pills to cool her down.

By the time Dolly was three years old, she decided to be more emphatic and make it known who really ruled the house. It came about when the owner wanted Dolly to get off the couch so he could stretch out. Dolly absolutely refused. When the owner did not stop bothering her and disturbing her peace by repeating his unreasonable request, Dolly answered with a deep growl accompanied by a snap. When that relentless man tried to remove her physically, Dolly bit him mercilessly.

Don't think this was an act of fear! Not with Dolly. She was not afraid at all, especially not of her owner. She merely wanted to prove her point and get her message across, "For heavens sake, leave me alone, I don't want to get off *my* couch, period!" As the owners did not have enough space for a second couch in their living room, and the husband did not enjoy lying on the floor, I got the chance to make the acquaintance of little Dolly the mighty dog and have an intimate eye-to-eye conversation with her ladyship for 10 weeks. That's how long it took her to understand once and forever that she was only a dog and supposed to serve her owners instead of the other way round.

Even Dolly's owners succeeded eventually in comprehending this fact. They had received a valuable lesson from their pet, and the contrast was too convincing to be neglected.

SUMMARY

1. The will-to-power varies in individual puppies. Some are born with a very high will-to-power, others with a lower one.
2. In selecting a puppy from a litter, note his assertiveness. A firm person will be better able to cope with a very assertive puppy than an easy-going person.
3. A puppy with an extra high will-to-power can already express his assertiveness to his owner at the early age of eight to ten weeks.
4. The will-to-power starts to grow around three to four months on the average.

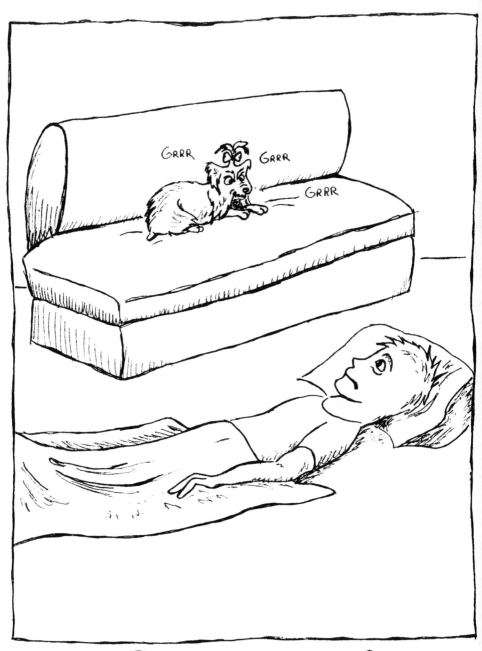

COMFORTABLE?

5. The higher the will-to-power of a puppy, the earlier the training should start.

6. Although it is not accepted or wanted behavior, it is natural for a dog to bite and express his will-to-power, especially when his survival instinct is triggered.

Re-Discovery of a Gene— The Dog's Innate Will-to-Serve

What is it that separates our domestic dog from wild canines including the wolf? What is so unique about man's best friend? It is the dog's second will, his serving nature, his eagerness to work for us and please us, his *will-to-serve.*

During the process of domestication, dogs came to recognize man as master and companion and to obey him. This was due to their innate desire to live in a socially defined structure controlled by a leader, which man became for them. The dog established a strong bond with him and developed a high degree of devotional attachment and loyalty toward man.

This innate will-to-serve has been an important asset in the domestication of the dog. Over numerous generations and centuries of coexistence the dog's will-to-serve became a genetic behavior imprint, which is present in no other domestic animal to such an extent on an unsolicited basis. It is really amazing to realize the variety of the dog's services to mankind:

1. Providing faithful and loyal companionship
2. Protecting our property and immediate family
3. Hunting and finding game for us
4. Retrieving game birds and rabbits for us
5. Herding and protecting our livestock
6. Acting as seeing-eye dogs
7. Acting as hearing-service dogs
8. Serving as companion dogs for the disabled
9. Locating and rescuing lost children in the wilderness and searching for people buried by avalanches and earthquakes
10. Assisting in police work and helping to discover hidden drugs
11. Saving us in various hazardous situations.

One of the many examples showing how a dog does not hesitate to sacrifice his life for the sake of his owner or another person is reflected in the following incidents:

An Irish setter was originally found dirty and hungry, and was adopted by the Donald Henderson family. The history is that Mr. and Mrs. Donald Henderson visited an auto dealer during the weekend and left their daughter in the back seat of their car with the dog Red.

All of a sudden, due to faulty wiring, a fire started in the car and smoke was pouring out of a slightly open front window. A salesman spotted it and alerted the parents.

Henderson raced out the door and before he could reach the car, he saw the dog exploding through the left rear window. The 75-pound setter touched the ground. Then he jumped up and reached back through the window of the car, grabbed Betty's coat collar with his teeth and dragged the girl out the broken window. She landed on her back and Red continued pulling her away from the burning car.

Woodie, a collie mix, was another canine hero.

One day, Rae Anne, her fiancé Ray, and Woodie were out hiking. Ray decided to photograph the view from atop a steep cliff nearby. As Rae Anne waited, Woodie began twisting and tugging, and Rae Anne realized something was wrong. She ran over the top of the hill and saw Ray lying face down, unconscious, in a stream 80 feet below. Suddenly, Woodie jerked the leash out of Rae Anne's hand and jumped over the cliff, breaking both her hips but nudging Ray's face out of the water, safe from drowning. She then began barking frantically for help.

Yes, the willingness of our domestic dogs to serve mankind is God's gift to us. Our share in this relationship is to understand the psychological needs of our dogs and train them with respect. Every dog, pure or mixed breed, is born with the genetic factor of this unique will-to-serve mankind. The initial level of the will-to-serve is influenced by individual differences depending on the overall personality of the dog. *Unlike the will-to-power, the will-to-serve does not grow automatically, but is directly affected by training.*

Lack of training or forceful training methods aimed at breaking the will-to-power can simultaneously destroy the will-to-serve. The will-to-serve can be compared with a muscle which atrophies without exercise or ruptures with improper exercise.

When dogs were mainly used to work for man and received the appropriate training, their serving nature was an important issue. The only dogs chosen for breeding were those which exhibited a high degree of servitude. Thus, this behavior imprint was intensified and maintained.

Because the dogs respected man as their master, they responded to his commands and would not harm people. The results of a series of genetic experiments to produce a special strain of German Shepherds, focused on a high working ability and beauty of conformation, at Fortunate Fields in Switzerland in the thirties prove this point convincingly:

"Despite the opinion prevailing among many people, teaching the German Shepherd to bite a man is the most difficult part of the police course. Certain, otherwise excellent, instructors are unable to make dogs attack. No amount of teasing seems able to overcome the dogs' prejudice against violating the person of man. Of the 67 dogs that failed in the police course because of the "unwillingness to bite at any cost," 62 of them earned average to high scores for their willingness in training." (E. Humphrey, L. Warner, 1934)

What is so amazing in this respect is that dogs with a higher willingness to work showed a greater refusal to attack and bite persons, and vice versa. This inbred respect and devotion was the reason why years ago, even rough handling by children could not make their pets bite.

Dogs were noted for their exceptional motivation to work willingly and voluntarily for a master with whom they had established this affectionate and devoted bond. Kind words and an occasional pat were sufficient rewards.

Unfortunately, this has changed completely over the past few decades. Compared to the overall number of dogs, the number of working dogs has declined. Recently dogs have been bred principally for conformation, for competition in shows, and as social companions. In the past, the breeding stock was of paramount importance regarding the intended use of the dog in order to preserve and maintain the specific traits of the breeding line. However, since the seventies I have observed a deterioration of the breed standards and a weakening of the genetic memory in certain breeds. Some individuals of particular breeds of hunting dogs did not show any interest in hunting or retrieving, Labradors were water-shy, and Retrievers were not eager to pick up a tossed dummy or ball.

I was contacted by a lady who owned an expensive three-year-old male Rottweiler who was supposed to be her watch dog. This dog just sat and, without interfering, watched a stranger taking down his owner's custom-built, walnut-planked, outdoor tub platform and cover, loading it on his pick-up truck and driving quietly away. A neighbor, who accidentally witnessed the incident, told the lady later that he had the impression the dog knew the thief and was his helper.

The lady assumed that buying an expensive working guard dog of an "intelligent breed" was the guarantee for specific bred-in performance. Also, she was not aware of the importance of conditioning through training to reinforce and maintain the desired behavior trait in the dog. As her experience and other examples prove, the breed standards are not always reliable.

Because the serving nature of the dog seems not to be an important genetic issue anymore for breeders, this very desirable trait has been largely diminished.

This fact, plus the overall lack of understanding regarding the necessity of early dog training, plus the general practice of forceful training, have directly contributed to the decline of the will-to-serve. As good or bad behavior patterns can be developed over a few generations, the consequence has been an annually increasing number of dog problems and bites.

Fortunately, there still exist some lines of certain breeds, e.g., German Shepherds, who do not even try to protect themselves or bite when they are mishandled with negative, forceful training methods. The genetic behavior of respect prevails.

The graph on Page 84 illustrates the typical development pattern of the will-to-serve in an untrained dog, relating the level to the age of the dog.

Usually, after the initial nearly constant phase of three months, the will-to-serve gradually starts to decrease if a dog does not receive any training. Up to seven months the downward trend is moderate whereas, between seven months and two years, it becomes more prominent. After an almost stagnant phase from two to three years it

FREE SPOT LABOR

lessens again until the age of four years and then maintains its level. (However, the will-to-serve can decline even faster if the dog is trained with improper methods involving punishment and pain.)

As a result of the steady decline of the will-to-serve, at a certain stage it drops below the level of the will-to-power. Then the will-to-power takes over. As a consequence, the dog starts to dominate his master rather than serving him. Instead of wanting to please, the dog demands to be pleased and only does what he likes out of self-gratification. Feeling in charge, the dog has no respect for people anymore and will hardly obey commands. Such a dog is a potential hazard, because he is unpredictable when he cannot have his way or something is not to his liking. He can be aggressive or destructive even without provocation, thus demonstrating his will-to-power.

Toby proved that to his owners very convincingly.

Toby's Story

Toby was a Rhodesian Ridgeback. These dogs, referred to as African Lion Hounds, were originally bred in South Africa for hunting in the wild. They are very strong and courageous.

Toby was acquired by her owners as an eight-week old puppy, about fifteen months before the couple's son Michael was born. From the beginning, Toby was a very sweet and affectionate pet and was treated as a child substitute—pampered, coddled, humanized and overwhelmed with emotional stimulation.

When Michael was born, he became the center of attention and Toby was relegated to a dog's life. However, she appeared not only to tolerate the situation but even seemed to love to play with the baby. Everybody had the impression that both were really fond of each other and everything went well for over a year.

Toby had never received any training. Her owners did not think that it was necessary to train her because the pet's behavior was generally quite acceptable for them.

Toby at birth had a low will-to-power of 2, but a high will-to-serve of 9. However, the will-to-serve gradually declined because Toby was not trained. At about 30 months the two wills clashed and the steadily growing will-to-power took over. That's when the behavior problems started. (See graph, Page 85)

The problems were not considered very serious in the beginning, but suddenly Toby's owners experienced a real shock.

One day they left her at home for about two hours and when they returned, they found Toby in their son Michael's room where she had gone berserk. She had done a very thorough job. There was blood all over the walls from her cut and bleeding mouth, the carpet was soaked with her excrement, toys were in pieces all over the place. Toby had completely flipped. But this was not the end of her rampage, just the beginning. One month later she destroyed the whole interior of the family car within half an hour. (See photo, Page 82)

Her owners' first reaction was to take her to the pound to have her put to sleep. Their fear was, if she could do this to their car, she could harm their child, too.

Her owners loved Toby very much and could not imagine having her destroyed. They also realized that they could not blame her for what she had done. Even more important, they were very much concerned about the safety and welfare of their son Michael. There was only one acceptable option for them—having her psychologically reprogrammed.

Based on the principle of mutual respect and structuring and disciplining Toby's mind, developing her willingness to please, without reprimand, punishment, or drugs, I cured Toby's rage syndrome. Her rehabilitation proved a complete success. Toby never took to the frenzy of chewing or destruction again, and remained a loving and safe companion for the family's son Michael for the remaining years of her life. (See photo, Page 82)

The *will-to-serve* can be stimulated in every dog with psychological training which does not destroy or suppress the will-to-power but uses it to support the will-to-serve.

Memories with Baroness

My well-trained champion Baroness had an extremely high will-to-power. However, she had also a very high will-to-serve. She would point and hunt for me from dawn to dusk without reservation.

One day, in working for a group of hunters, Baroness sprained her right front leg. Instead of giving up, she hunted for most of the day on

43

"Mrs. B."

Baroness Meisterfeld CDX-CDA, N.G.S.P.R.C., N.G.S.P.N.P.B.R.C.

Translation: AKC Companion Dog Excellent (Obedience, Canine Distinction Award (Recorded in the Dog Hall of Fame) for AKC Obedience.

National German Shorthair Pointer Retriever Champion (she earned a perfect 500 score and held the title for 1962, 1963 and 1964.)

Baroness also won the National German Shorthair Pointer Association National German Pointing Breeds Retriever Championship in 1964.

three legs. She was never a quitter; whatever she set on doing was completed.

I remember the first time she saw a deer. It was our first summer in California. We were hiking in a state park in Marin County. Baroness was not on a hunt command. She just stayed on the path 10 to 15 yards in front of me testing the various scents. Suddenly she locked up on a solid point. I instinctively stopped. Baroness had been trained to freeze on point when she winded or saw a pheasant and wait for my command. I "whoad" her and looked in the direction of her head, which she used as a pointer. There was no growth along the path, and she was pointing straight down it. Then I saw a deer standing about 100 yards in front of us. For a couple of minutes we all looked each other over. I had never seen a deer this close in Ohio, and Baroness had never seen a deer at all.

Baroness stayed on point, and for the first time in her six years of hunting with me, she began to tremble. A hidden genetic memory must have been stirred in her. German Shorthair Pointers are known to hunt for both feather and fur. However, I had never experienced her freezing on point when she encountered horses in the field trials, or cows, sheep and goats in the pastures.

As the deer walked around the bend another 200 feet away, he disappeared from view. I thought, "What the heck, she needs to exercise, and she will never catch the deer anyway." So I gave her the command "fetch." She was gone like an arrow from a bow. She flew across the path, around the bend, and was out of sight. Again, as I am looking back, I have to admit, it was a foolish thing to do, because I did know my dog so well.

I followed her direction, and just before I reached the bend, I heard Baroness' voice. This was very strange to my ears, since she was a silent tracker when we hunted Ohio's "cotton tails" (rabbits). What I was hearing was a baying sound, which was familiar to me from my hunting nights with racoon dogs.

I broke out in a run. When I turned the bend I froze. Ahead of me was a scene I will never forget. The deer was down on his side, Baroness had her front paws on the deer's right shoulder. When he tried to rise, she grabbed him by the throat and growled. Obviously this was a relic of her German heritage when these dogs were bred for hunting deer.

I rushed to the scene and looked the deer over. I saw lots of saliva on the deer's neck, none on his mouth, so I assumed it must have been hers. There was no sign of injury or blood, just the sight of a frightened deer, of a conquering dog, and an amazed owner.

I gave Baroness the "leave it" command. She willingly and obediently backed off, even though this must have been the thrill of her lifetime. And the deer? He got up, ran about 100 yards, and then slowly walked away.

SUMMARY

1. The extent of the willingness to please and work for man is what separates our domestic dog from the rest of the animal kingdom.
2. The uniqueness of the will-to-serve is the main reason why dog breeders of yesteryears enhanced certain behavior traits in the dog through selective breeding aimed at his greater usefulness for man.
3. Originally, each breed of dogs had a certain functional serving/working task to perform.
4. Because all breeds (including cross/mixed breeds) have this unique will-to-serve and innate loyalty toward mankind, using our animal wrath to train the dog with forceful methods must be considered a wrong and shameful act.

Genetic Behavior Overruled — Chindo's Story

The innate will-to-serve and work for mankind, as the most important genetic behavior trait of the dog to man, can not only control the will-to-power, but also other natural instincts, and can even be developed to be stronger than other inherited traits. By conditioning the will-to-serve, the dog becomes able to control such genetic behavior patterns as his chasing instinct and inbred fighting instinct.

Chindo is a living example of how genetic behavior patterns can be not only overridden but can even be changed through learning, thanks to the uniqueness of the-will-to serve.

Major Jack Craft became aware of and interested in the Chindo breed shortly after his arrival in Korea in 1969. The Chindo is the national dog of Korea, originating in the little island of Chindo off the

Southwest coast. These dogs are noted for their loyalty, adaptability, cunning, and intelligence, paired with fighting spirit, hunting ability and a reputation as ratters.

The major got his genuine Chindo as a seven-week old male puppy. This puppy was completely different from any other puppy he and his family had ever owned. For example, he was already housebroken by his Chindo mother. From the beginning he maintained a rigid set of behavior standards for himself, which the major had never before observed in a dog. The puppy would not eat stale food or table scraps and ate only at night. No other animal was tolerated near his food. He accepted human intrusion, however. The most unusual thing about this pup was that no other dog could dominate him. He never gave in, or begged, or ran. He was very independent and quite aggressive with the other dogs and animals in the neighborhood.

Chindo grew into a beautiful dog of 50 pounds. He loved to hunt, especially rats, but hated loud noises and car rides. When he was kept on a leash or in the house, Chindo was submissive, a warm and friendly dog. He never gave more than a warning growl or bark at a stranger because he respected man. He had a different attitude toward animals, however, demonstrating the animal world belonged to him.

When he was an eight-month old puppy, he was threatened by a full-grown hunting dog. He immediately had the hound on his back, slashing him open before holding him by his throat. One day the major lost his temper with Chindo and grabbed him by the flank, a spot about which the dog had always been very protective. Chindo snapped at him. The major did not want a biter as a family dog, but a dog he could walk comfortably—one that would obey him and not try to attack or challenge other animals. Therefore, he arranged for his psychological reprogramming.

Training Chindo was a new experience for me, because he was so different from any other dog that I had ever encountered. Chindo was not a "macho" dog with something to prove. For Chindo, fighting was a way of life—as natural as wagging his tail.

To prevent Chindo's fighting instinct from being triggered by facing living objects, he was kept in a specially designed run with a panelled front gate and sides to block the view of other dogs and the deer that lived and grazed in our fields.

In the beginning of his training program my first step was to slowly

47

develop a communication with him through basic obedience. This was later complemented by some special commands. I then succeeded in walking him around the ranch animals without having him show any interest in them. One time I was walking Chindo in our field looking for a sitting jack rabbit. My intention was to startle the rabbit and when he began to run, to give Chindo his special command "leave it." Chindo was properly heeling, but all of a sudden, like a lighting bolt, he advanced and seized a gopher snake, gave it one snap, shook it, and tossed it out of our way. Then within the same moment he fell back into the heel position. All this happened so fast that I stood there for a couple of minutes before I could fully understand what had taken place. I had never before, or since, experienced a dog moving with such speed.

A harder, more time-consuming task, was to persuade Chindo to leave dogs alone, because of his inherited instinct to challenge any dog that encroached on "his" territory. Therefore, it was extremely difficult for him to understand that it was wrong to attack other dogs. It was very hard on him too, considering the conflict of his desire to please me with his natural impulse to fight.

Fortunately, his will to please was so high that he was able to overcome his genetic and conditioned instinct to fight four-legged animals. It was a painstakingly slow process (three months of therapy training) until Chindo had finally learned not to react to aggressive, challenging dogs. A crucial point in this whole procedure was that Chindo was never physically punished for his fighting tendency.

The major and his family were very pleased with their "new" Chindo. One day he called me and proudly related an incident that had just taken place. He had put Chindo on a down-stay command in his back yard when his attention was diverted by a visiting neighbor. Some time had passed in conversation when all at once the major remembered he had left Chindo unsupervised. He hurried over to where he had left Chindo in the most vulnerable position for a dog, especially a fighting dog, just in time to witness a German Shepherd giving Chindo the sniff test. Chindo merely glanced at the dog and laid his head on his paws. The major gave Chindo the "be good" command (to be on the safe side) before chasing the German Shepherd away. He then praised Chindo lavishly. Perhaps that was Chindo's greatest victory.

Next, an adopted female beagle was accepted by Chindo as part of the family. They even played together. A Siamese cat was another happy addition to the household. Chindo lived in friendship and peace with these animals and remained an amazing, beautiful, living proof that it is possible to transform a merciless fighter into a gentle friend and protector. (See photos, Page 81)

SUMMARY
1. The will-to-serve can be used to overrule genetic behavior as shown by the case of Chindo.
2. It was natural for Chindo to fight and kill because he was bred for this purpose.
3. When his owner attempted to punish Chindo, triggering his survival instinct, it was natural for him to bite in self-defense.
4. Instead of using force and punishment in his reprogramming, which would have compounded Chindo's problem, his willingness to please was properly developed. It then could control his will-to-power and strongly inbred fighting instinct.

The Discriminating Mind

Another facet of the dog's personality and behavior is his discriminating mind, which works through his five external senses of smell, sight, hearing, touch, and taste. The intensity of the external senses differs widely in various breeds and individual dogs. However, the sensory equipment of all dogs is extraordinary and should be taken into account when we are relating to them.

For safety reasons and with regard to the training we administer to our dogs, it is very important to understand how a dog operates in this respect—how via the *orientation reflex* a dog perceives and explores any stimulus, and how his body responds with an *adaptation reflex*, depending on the kind of stimulus perceived.

The preferred way for a dog to discriminate is through his sense of smell. His smelling capacity is about 500 times better than ours. His olfactory sense and his excellent memory for smells enable a dog to analyze a vast number of odors, more than a thousand different kinds of scents, and to make a distinction among them. A dog explores the world with his nose. He can smell animals and people from a great distance and follow tracks which are several days old.

His second important sense is his hearing ability. His hearing greatly surpasses ours. A dog can hear a greater range of sounds, with a higher frequency and pitch, and from a greater distance. For instance, the dog reacts to the signal of a Galton whistle which we are not able to hear at all. The dog can also very accurately localize a sound's point of origin and discern the slightest differences in tone. For this reason, a dog is very negatively affected by angry shouting and sudden, loud noises.

His excellent hearing ability enables the dog to understand our words and commands even when articulated with a very low voice. If a dog is well-trained, he can understand up to eighty words on an average. However, a very intelligent dog can be taught as many as 400 words and to interpret their different meanings with a precise response, but this is considered exceptional.

Thanks to his excellent hearing capacity, it is completely sufficient to give commands in a soft tone of voice. Especially after the dog is already alerted, he should be calmed with comforting and soothing sounds which do not convey an additional challenge for him.

Regarding sight, it has been established that a dog has a wider angle of vision and can see farther than we do. He can also see far better in the dark. However, a dog cannot distinguish colors as well as we do. He watches our facial expressions, especially our eyes and body movements, and interprets them. This also holds true for observation of other dogs or animals. Any of our gestures, postures, or facial expressions which are hostile according to the dog's code, such as making sudden, jerky movements, can incite an alarm reaction in the dog. Staring at a dog can trigger an adverse response because that is how dogs challenge one another.

The dog's sense of touch is comparable with ours. He has about the same threshold for pain, but he is more sensitive to electric shocks, as the salt content of his blood is higher. Intense stroking leads to adrenal stimulation and sexual excitement in the dog.

The sense of taste is of secondary importance because a dog gulps his food and relies more on his smelling capacity. That is why dogs easily fall victim to poisoned food and should be protected from possible harm in this respect.

Considering a dog's high sensitivity, all training methods conveying a visual threat and connected with any kind of physical punishment trigger the survival instinct indelibly.

SUMMARY

1. The dog's most developed sense is his smell. It is his preferred way to discriminate objects, animals, and people.
2. Because his hearing ability is superior to ours, shouting and other loud noises produced to reprimand a dog have a very negative effect on him.
3. Because a dog observes us closely, we should abstain from threatening gestures and not gaze at him. He could interpret these as hostile acts and retaliate.
4. A dog is sensitive to pain. Hitting and shocking affect him strongly and are inhumane methods to correct him.

Discrimination Safety Period

When a dog registers different external stimuli with his senses, they are transmitted via nerve fibers to special sections in his brain and filed away within a fraction of a second. The response is usually automatic. What happens, for example, when a dog meets a stranger?

During the discrimination process, especially within the first 15 seconds, the dog is in a state of alert. This is manifested by the high surge of adrenal flow through his whole body. The body becomes tense, the tail stiffens, the signals of danger. If the dog receives pleasant or familiar impressions, the adrenals quiet down in the time frame of 15 to 30 seconds and the dog starts to relax. Between 30 to 45 seconds the adrenal reaction has nearly or completely ceased. However, it is safer to wait another 15 seconds, i.e., up to a minute, before establishing the first contact with a strange dog, provided he exhibits friendliness.

If the impressions are unpleasant or unfamiliar, the dog remains alert and his adrenals are further stimulated. Because his survival instinct is activated, the dog is inclined to react with flight or aggression, depending on his will-to-power.

Based on these facts, it becomes obvious why a dog may bite even familiar persons when surprised or startled by them. He did not have enough time to discriminate and decide "friend or foe." As this mechanism of discrimination is always in force, caution is also advised with your own pet. When the dog is sleeping, he should not be petted suddenly. He also should not be approached by surprise and touched

51

Hazardous Improper Approach

Right Approach

from behind. Instead, when you call his name first, you give him the opportunity to recognize you acoustically and visually, permitting him to make a complex discrimination. (See chart, DISCRIMINA-TION SAFETY PERIOD, Page 85) When a friend wants to introduce a dog to you, let the owner come to you with the dog on leash. Carefully present the back of your closed hand to the dog to permit him to record your scent. Never reach out with an open hand with your fingers extended because this could result in a bite due to fear. The dog could perceive this as a threat, especially if he is accustomed to being punished with the hand. It is much easier for a dog to get hold of your outstretched fingers compared to the back of your fist.

SUMMARY

1. When meeting a strange dog it is important to allow the dog time to discriminate.
2. The signals to beware are when a dog's body tenses and his tail stiffens.
3. During the first 15 seconds the adrenal flow through a dog's body is very high.
4. Allow up to one minute for the adrenals to quiet down before you touch your friend's dog.
5. When you are in doubt whether you should establish contact with a strange dog, **DON'T!**

BETTER to be SAFE than SORRY!

The Role of the Adrenals

Under normal conditions, the adrenal glands are quiet. When a dog perceives a threat (loud noise, strange person, threatening body gestures, etc.) the adrenal secretions are pumped into the system. The dog is ready to run, defend, or attack.

The chart on Page 88 shows how the adrenals can be stimulated. One way is by fear—by yelling, hitting, scaring with the throw-can or whistle described later. They can also be stimulated by projecting feelings of anger toward a dog, because he can sense our emotions.

Another way the adrenals can be activated is through emotional conditioning. This may take the form of gushy, smothering praise, usually accompanied by high-pitched baby talk and lots of stroking.

It is a common experience of groomers that, when dog owners make a huge fuss over their pets before leaving them at the grooming shop ("Oh don't worry my little darling, Mommy will be back real soon. You be good now..."), giving them a lot of hugs and petting, the dogs will be hyped up and extremely difficult to groom. Yet when others were brought in and left just as a matter of fact ("See you later, Sammy."), the dogs were calmer and no problem to groom.

Here are three of the main factors that influence the direction of the flight/fight response based on the adrenal reaction:

1. *Will-to-Power*
   A dog with a very high will-to-power is more likely to either stand his ground or become aggressive when feeling threatened. A dog with a low will-to-power will exhibit fear and try to escape.
2. *Age*
   A puppy is more likely to exhibit the flight response because his will-to-power is usually low during the younger stages, and he is less sure of himself than an older dog. However, there are many examples in which puppies, only a few months old will charge when they have a very high will-to-power.
3. *Past Experiences*
   Very often a flight response will, in time, reverse itself and become a fight response. This happens through a series of minor conquests making the dog bolder until he becomes the aggressor.

How can this behavior be changed? Sometimes the aggressive fight response can be changed or modified using negative reinforcement (punishment). However, we may find that the negative reinforcement must be reapplied periodically in order to maintain the correct behavior. Then there are some dogs that will only get more aggressive when punishment is used. The question here is, how do you know whether this method will improve your dog's behavior or make it worse? I know many dog owners who have been bitten finding out.

What about the dog that is operating on the flight response? In this case, using any form of negative reinforcement will only compound the problem.

The story of Sasha confirms how a flight response can reverse itself into a fight response.

Sasha

Sasha's owners acquired her when she was six weeks old. Their veterinarian pronounced Sasha a "beautiful, healthy puppy." The owners happily took their new puppy home and proceeded to pamper and spoil her.

By the time Sasha was three months old, her behavior was starting to get out of control. When the situation had not improved by the time Sasha turned five months, the owner decided to call the breeder to ask for advice.

The breeder suggested that if hitting or yelling at the dog did not work, they should get a plastic container, fill it half full with gravel, and without warning, throw it near the dog. The noise was supposed to shock her out of misbehaving. The owners took this advice, but observed that the use of the throw/shake can was making Sasha more nervous and increasingly fearful.

When she was seven months old, a change began taking place in Sasha's behavior. Her owners noticed that instead of reacting fearfully to visitors and situations, she was becoming more and more aggressive. Her size had made it even more difficult to control her. At this time the owners decided to have Sasha spayed. This proved to be an ordeal, not only for the dog, but for the veterinarian as well.

When the owners went to pick up their dog, they were not prepared for the diagnosis they received from the vet. He informed them that Sasha's aggression was not normal for a puppy, and that she was vicious, paranoid and very dangerous. He went on to say that as Sasha continued to grow, she would be extremely difficult to control, and that she would seriously hurt someone someday. He then advised putting Sasha to sleep.

The owners left Sasha with me for rehabilitation training.

At the end of her 11-week program, Sasha's behavior had undergone dramatic, positive changes. The change was so great that she appeared on live-television with me (Channel 13, Stockton, CA).

If ever there was an occasion to justify a dog's flight or fight response, it is in a television studio. However, amid the confusion of lights, noise, cameras, and strangers Sasha remained calm and in control. She merely observed the activities with interest and a wagging tail.

In my opinion, disciplining and structuring a dog's mind through psychological conditioning with only positive reinforcement, is the most effective (and safest) way to reduce the stress of prior negative conditioning and normalize a dog's behavior. This means exercising, developing, and conditioning the dog's willingness to work for us and please us. It is truly the key to controlling the flight or fight response. Try it. Your dog will love you for it.

SUMMARY
1. The adrenal system supports the dog's survival instinct.
2. The more sensitive a dog is, the easier it is to trigger his flight or fight response.
3. The fearful, flight-preferring young dog can later become an aggressive, fighting dog.
4. The adrenals are conditioned by either fear-causing stimuli or emotional stimulation such as gushy talk and lots of stroking.
5. Fear-causing stimuli such as hitting, scaring with sounds like yelling and throw can are prone to make your dog paranoid and very dangerous, like Sasha.

The Territorial Mind

Dogs have a very sensitive attitude regarding territorial boundaries. Because they feel threatened, most dogs will react aggressively and bite when their territorial safety region is invaded. Their most critical zone, the personal safety range, is about 5 to 8 feet, where a dog feels within the reach of an adversary. Their general territorial zone is 15 to 20 feet. It is their flight distance. The more fearful a dog, the greater the flight distance he needs. At a certain point he will retreat, at another he will attack when a person or animal he perceives as hostile is within his critical territory.

When a dog feels cornered and has no possible avenue to escape, he will become very frightened and act in self-defense on the spot, either by giving a warning signal with a growl, or by biting immediately without warning. Therefore, it is very dangerous to try to pet a strange dog in a car or a dog tied up or confined in a yard. Most dogs take their job of guarding their owner's property *very* seriously and express that by barking and/or biting when a stranger enters their territory.

While a dog is feeding he may respond aggressively as his owner approaches due to his territorial sensitivity. If the owner condones the dog's threatening attitude he actually strongly conditions this territorial demand of the dog. The owner should never accept this behavior from his dog, but instead he should desensitize his pet in this respect.

Dogs are generally more aggressive on their own territory. Some dogs extend their safety zone over the critical distance of about 15 to 20 feet no matter where they are. Stepping into a dog's safety range always involves risks.

Our domestic dogs have a psychological need for their owners to define the territorial boundaries for them. This includes physical (house, yard) and psychological (in a behavioral sense) boundaries. This need separates man's best friend from the rest of the animal kingdom, including the wolf. Of paramount importance is that training to establish the territorial limits should take place as soon as the puppy comes into your home and before it is four to five months old. Thus, a lot of behavior problems can be prevented. Otherwise, due to the dog's developing learning ability, he self-teaches based on his daily experiences of self-gratification and adrenal stimulation. If uncontrolled, his territorial boundaries are constantly expanding. First, his home/yard is his domain to be protected. Then the next-door neighbor's yard, followed by one to several city blocks, are integrated into his territory. In his kingdom he will challenge any intruder, be it four-legged or human.

The story of Keno illustrates how a lack of training and territorial boundaries can transform a delightful Labrador puppy into a vagabond with an ever-growing territorial expansion drive, without any respect for limits and boundaries.

Keno

Keno belonged to my closest neighbor. He was kept outside the yard most of each day while his owner was at work. Not content to stay by himself, Keno plotted ways of escaping his confinement and boredom.

At first, forays to my property and back lot satisfied his needs and curiosity. Next, the surrounding pastures full of sheep and dairy herds provided this free-roaming dog with much more excitement and temptation.

When I became aware of what was happening to Keno, I mentioned to my neighbor that I was witnessing changes in the dog's behavior. Some basic obedience training should not be harmful to the pet. But the neighbor did not think that was necessary. "Keno will outgrow this. I want him to enjoy his puppyhood."

Keno became a professional wanderer. The lovely, sweet-natured puppy grew into a hyperactive, sometimes groveling dog. On the loose, both a constant surplus of scent and visual stimulation conditioned him to increased indulgence and excitability. Keno chased whatever he bumped into and barked at whatever moved. He displayed a total lack of discipline as he made his daily rounds of an ever-increasing territory.

By five months of age, Keno's territory covered the next door rancher's pasture land of 50 acres. By six months, he was a regular visitor at the school two miles away, having his adrenals stimulated by romping with the school children in the playground. Sometimes he followed the children into the classroom, resulting in a call to the owner's wife and a car ride home.

Keno had no sense of proportion regarding his territory. Punishment did not prove effective in keeping him home. It was mostly a matter of good luck that he did not get lost, was not hit by a car, or shot by a rancher fearing for his endangered livestock.

Fortunately, the owner eventually did realize the necessity for some discipline in Keno's life through training and brought him to me. When placed in one of our runs, however, suddenly his two-mile plus territory was reduced to a five by twenty foot space. Keno's stress was immediate and obvious. He whined, howled, barked and cried for three solid days grieving for the loss of his dominion. But at least he was on his way to a cure.

"I DARE YOU"

Territorial Protectiveness

A serious problem in connection with the dog's territorial protectiveness is that our mail carriers employed with the U.S. Postal Service, United Parcel, and Federal Express, as well as other service personnel such as meter readers, etc., are experiencing an increasing number of dog attacks and bites.

A young lady who enjoyed her job as a mail carrier very much and had loved dogs all her life told me what she had experienced recently:

"When I was inserting mail in a family's mailbox where I had delivered mail for quite some time without problems, I was suddenly attacked by a dog who came from behind the house. Even though I managed to prevent being bitten and to slowly back out of the yard, this negative experience left a deep scar in my mind. Although the Postal Service issued a warning to the dog's owner after this incident, saying the mail delivery would be subject to confinement of the dog, I turned in my resignation within two weeks. They offered me an inside position in which I was not interested. I had taken the carrier job for the outdoor experience and the walking exercise which now I was unable to continue due to my fear. My problem is that I cannot help but recall this ferocious dog flying at me with all four feet off the ground. It is like a recurring nightmare. I become almost paranoid when I encounter a dog, and so does my eight-year old son, whom I unfortunately infected with my fear."

SUMMARY
1. Every dog is territorial.
2. The most critical territorial range for a dog, his personal safety zone, is within five to eight feet.
3. When a dog feels cornered with no avenue to escape and becomes fearful, he will bite...even his owner.
4. Every dog has the psychological need for his owner to define for him territorial and behavioral limits, and to condition him through training.
5. Without training, the dog's physical and behavioral boundaries will constantly expand until there are no more limits.
6. When you permit your dog to define his own boundary lines, he can become a hazard to service personnel who need to enter your property.

7. Being surprised by such an overly protective dog can be a traumatic experience for life. The affected service person can transmit this phobia to other family members, including children.

Reasoning

So much has been written about whether dogs can reason.

Several well-known behaviorists expressed the opinion that animals, including dogs, cannot reason because they lack words and names for things. How about a person, born deaf and mute, who has never had the chance to go to a special school, and has never heard or learned any articulate expressions? Then some human beings should not be able to reason, either...

As dogs have a mind, memory, senses, feelings, and emotions, they are able to form mental pictures of their environment. They store them and make associations based on their instincts, intelligence, conditioning, and experiences.

It has been a great advantage that a dog's instincts have become weaker in the process of domestication. Because of this, instead of following his basic instincts in a hostile way in a given situation, he *acts* in a responsible manner according to his training.

In my opinion, dogs do have the capacity to reason, to a certain extent. This is directly related to their intelligence, experience, motivation, and amount and quality of training. They are not capable of the complex thought processes or advance planning of human beings. However, they can evaluate a given object, situation, or event and make a certain decision from multiple choices, that is *not* necessarily stereotyped, even when they are conditioned to form a given response. There is no doubt that dogs understand what they have learned, remember it, and apply their learning experience later, in demanding, related situations. But they do more than that by creatively varying and adjusting this learned behavior to ever-changing situations.

It is well known that dogs communicate with each other, and also communicate with us, despite the fact that we are often deaf and blind to their signals, or misinterpret them due to a lack of knowledge. Dogs have proven their great ability to learn to understand our signals, comprehend the meaning of our words, read our body language, and interpret the expressions of our feelings.

How many people have experienced occasions when their dog did something wrong and afterwards seemed to express a kind of guilt feeling even without ever being punished before for such an offense? Or how dogs try to mask a wrongdoing by pretending to have nothing to do with it? Dogs are true con-artists, which involves, in my opinion, a certain amount of reasoning.

During decades around dogs I have been confronted with numerous examples of their skills in this respect. They use their reasoning ability in many ways, to manipulate people and exploit situations to their own advantage, but also in their service for mankind.

A very good example is Seeing Eye dogs. They learn to scan and evaluate the surroundings in order to prevent probable dangers for their handicapped masters. Every day they have to show initiative, make decisions and "think things out" for the person they lead. They have to intelligently disobey or obey commands depending on the situation they have to cope with. They do it focused on the safety aspect of their guide task. The same applies to sled dogs. In many instances, the life of their master depends on their skills and reasoning ability in hazardous situations. It is fascinating how sled dogs cancel the sled driver's command if it is hazardous, such as continuing to lead over a crevice or thin ice that could not support the weight of the sled team.

In my long-time work with dogs I have found that the more extensively and better trained a dog is, the more improved his potential for further learning and successfully completing more and more complex tasks requiring a certain amount of reasoning.

My dog Baroness was an outstanding example.

Baroness

One of the tests a dog must go through in a retrieving trial is called a "blind retrieve." The dog is placed behind a four-foot-high, free-standing "blind," which is comparable to a folding panel screen. The handler watches over the blind as the bird is placed in the cover across the duck pond. He is then required to send his dog across the water and, using directional signals, guide the dog to the planted bird.

When I was first training my German Shorthair Pointer Baroness for these trials, I parked my station wagon parallel to the riverbank and used it as an improvised blind. I gave Baroness a sit-stay command on the side of the car away from the river, about a foot away from the driver's door, facing it. Then I hopped in my boat, rowed across the river, placed a training bumper in the high weeds and rowed back. I took Baroness down to the river and gave her an "across" command. Once on the other side, I directed her to the bumper location. After she had retrieved the bumper and delivered it to me, I would repeat the process, hiding the bumper in a different spot each time.

Baroness loved nothing more than to hunt in this way, and within a few days she was doing exceptionally well on the blind retrieves. I marveled at how she seemed to anticipate my directions. It appeared she didn't even need any handling. She was almost...well, too good. I began to notice that she always swam straight for the bumper, no matter where I hid it. It was not possible that she could have tracked me through the water.

I decided to test her by rowing downwind and concealing the bumper under some river debris along the opposite bank. I rowed back and walked up the bank to get Baroness. She was sitting in her usual place facing the car door. I took her down to the water and sent her off. Without any handling on my part, Baroness swam straight to where I had hidden the bumper, dug it out of the debris and brought it back to me.

I was trying to figure out how she knew exactly where to go on a blind retrieve when my neighbor hailed me from next door.

"Did you see Baroness just now, Joe?" I asked. "She found that bumper all by herself! She's either reading my mind or she has x-ray eyes."

Joe laughed. "Neither one," he said. "I saw the whole thing and I think that dog o'yours is smarter'n you are. When you got in the boat, she dropped down on all fours and watched from underneath the car. When you got in the boat to come back, she sat up again."

I guess, she was smarter than I was, at that!

"One very important attribute of animal behavior that seems intuitively to suggest conscious thinking is its adaptability to changing circumstances." (Griffin, 1984)

SUMMARY
1. Dogs have a limited capacity to reason.
2. Their reasoning process deals with the "now time" and not with

the complexity of abstract future events.

3. As we have to educate our children to develop their abilities, our pets' minds need to be trained too.
4. The more and better you train your dog (without force and punishment), the more reasonable his performance in critical situations.

Sense Perception

It is not easy to define sense perception and to prove it with practical examples. I see sense perception as an intuitive knowingness beyond the five senses, but supported by them. Sense perception is inherent in all creatures.

When I watched the quail which come for food to the glass door of my living room, I noticed a Siamese cat in their immediate feeding area only about four feet away. The quail were not at all afraid, because this cat is a pure mouser. They just looked at him and seemed to scold him because he was in their territory. The cat calmly walked away. I observed the same when a black-and-white cat approached them.

I thought, "What is wrong with my quail? Don't they have any sense of self-preservation anymore?" These questions were answered, when a grey cat showed up. The quail immediately took refuge in the bushes and trees.

The quail showed similar behavior with prey birds. They did not react at all to buzzards, but if a hawk was in the vicinity they were already hiding, even though the bird was high up and cast no shadow.

It is well-known that a high-spirited horse can, at the moment his rider mounts, already sense whether the person is an experienced rider, regardless of his body weight.

I have also encountered this incredible sense perception with my goat Matthew, a Nubian. When I presented a problem dog to him with an aggressive background that was not obvious, he would rise on his hind legs. A highly aggressive dog made him rise completely, almost six feet tall! In other words, the level of his rising was an indicator for, and directly proportional to, the amount of aggressiveness in the dogs I had for evaluation. This was confirmed by the owner's written case history and other tests.

After I had reprogrammed the dogs for about three months I presented them a second time to Matthew for a final test. Matthew would not rise a bit, because the dogs were not aggressive anymore and had become friendly and social. He even permitted the dogs to come up and sniff him. So I could completely rely on Matthew's diagnosis.

My Koi carp in the little indoor pond inside the training ring showed the same accurate responses. When I walked up to the pond with an aggressive dog, they would swim to the farthest corner of the pond and hide. Yet the same dog after reprogramming did not cause them to move an inch, even when the dog drank water from the spot in the pond where they were.

It was interesting to observe that dogs brought to me with behavior problems other than aggression did not elicit a reaction either from my goat or from the carp in the pond.

This very precise perceiving ability can often be observed when a dog owner permits his dog to join a group of visiting friends. Usually the dog goes around to greet everybody, but will sometimes by-pass a person; and regardless of the encouragement he receives, he will avoid that particular person.

Another interesting observation my clients have made is that when they turned their dog over to a conformation handler for A.K.C. showing, the dog suddenly became well mannered and performed excellently, even though the dog had never met the handler before. The dog sensed the master in the handler.

I have heard from many of my clients that their dog just seems to know that a car ride will end up at the vet's. All of a sudden their dog disappears even though they create the sound the dog loves most— the jingling of the car keys.

How can the dog find out if he does not sense it?

SUMMARY
1. Sense perception is an intuitive knowingness beyond the five senses.
2. Dogs can sense the mental and emotional states of their owners not only in their presence but also when separated from them by distance.
3. Because of the dog's "sense-ability" it is not advisable for an owner, who is in a state of emotional turmoil, angry, or busy with other things, to train his dog. This can affect the dog very negatively and impair the success of training.

66

CHAPTER III

DOG PROBLEMS—EVALUATION OF THE EVIDENCE

Testing of Dogs and Analysis of Their Problems

Now that we have discussed the various facets of the dog's personality, it becomes obvious how many different aspects must be considered when a dog causes problems. It is not sufficient just to examine the negative symptoms a problem dog exhibits in his behavior in order to reprogram him. Besides the symptoms, the nature of the detrimental influences has to be identified.

Therefore, my basic approach to psychological reprogramming is to determine the cause of the behavioral problems and then to establish the foundation for rehabilitation.

The analytical procedure starts immediately during the phone conversation with the owner(s) (husband and wife):

What are their basic attitudes? Do they already have "all the answers" as to the cause of their dog's problem? If they do, then there is no merit in consulting with them. All they are seeking is a professional to agree with their philosophy. Dog owners with such an attitude are seldom prepared to accept new concepts and valuable advice and to integrate them into their relationship with their dog. A reprogramming of their pet would be in vain. They would continue their old ways, and the pet would have no choice but to revert to his former behavior patterns caused and ingrained by this old environment in order to fit into it. Mr. Trumbull was one of them.

Princess, My Love

It always surprises me when clients who are paying me for professional advice refuse it. The more I point out and explain the logical reasons for the problems they are facing with their dog, the more they rebel. Any time I express a contradictory opinion to their way of thinking, they will disagree. They take pains to avoid admitting the truth.

PRINCESS MY LOVE

When I showed Mr. Trumbull the illustrations of the different kinds of relationships in HOWS & WHYS OF PSYCHOLOGICAL DOG TRAINING, at the third picture he burst out laughing. "Look at that! That's her, that's my princess, no doubt about it! The first day I brought her home she acted like a royal princess. I had to call her 'Princess.'

"Do you know, I could not get her to eat dog food from the beginning. She likes baked chicken best. Of course, I take out all the bones ahead of time."

Mr. Trumbull's face was beaming with pride and excitement when he described the various food dishes he prepared for his Princess.

"The only dish I wish she wouldn't like that much is kidneys. You know, you have to boil the pi.. out of them before they are really tender. Princess would never touch them when they are still a little tough. And man, do they smell up the house. Every time I have to use spray freshener and open the windows to get rid of the stink!"

With all the rituals he went through with cooking for his dog, and his stubborn belief that this was the only way to go, he pushed my button. With my remark: "Mr. Trumbull, you really don't have to go to all that trouble to feed Princess. It really isn't necessary," I jumped right into the pot of boiling kidneys. All of a sudden, his face turned dark. All the beaming light was gone. Before I could add something comforting he burst out, "What do *you* know about what I went through? If it weren't for my cooking, Princess would already have starved to death. In the beginning, I was so foolish as to take the advice of the breeder, and I fed her only Kibble. But she would not even touch that dog stuff. For two whole days Princess did not eat anything, can you imagine? No sir, Princess needs that special diet I'm preparing her. And I do not need any advice on her feeding. As you can see, her coat is shiny, and her nose is moist."

"Mr. Trumbull, what I was leading into is that catering to her will not give you control. If anything, this only enhances the behavior problems you are experiencing with her."

I paused. I wanted that to sink in. Sometimes, when a client gets his emotions riled, logic has a difficult time being accepted. And this was one of the sometimes.

"Excuse me, I'll be right back. I need to let a dog out." With that I left Mr. Trumbull in my office to think it out. Whee, I guess I was in need of a break even more than he.

As I sat back down in my office chair, I picked up a piece of chalk from my desk. "Maybe a couple of pictures would help you to understand what I'm trying to explain to you." With that I illustrated the present relationship between Princess and him.

"Look Mr. Trumbull, Princess needs her boundaries established. There is no way around that."

"How long will it take you to train her, so I can have control over her? I really don't mind her jumping on me and growling when I try to get her off the bed in order to make it up. What I can't live with, and what I'm most concerned about, is her running after and chasing kids on bicycles."

"I don't remember that you told me Princess was growling at you. How long has that been going on?"

"Oh, only about three or four months. But I can understand her very well, because I would probably growl and snap also, if someone was pushing me off my favorite comfortable bed."

"Mr. Trumbull, if you really want to have her trained, it would be necessary to change all these negative behaviors, including her dislike of being told to move. As a matter of fact, one of the main things when she got back home would be for her not to get up on any furniture at all, period! What is needed to control her is a complete change, even to the point of a different name."

"A different name? For whom?"

"Your dog, of course."

"What's her name got to do with her behavior? I don't see the connection. Are you putting me on? Maybe *you* need a shrink!"

I thought, maybe I do after all. Most dog trainers just train their clients' dogs and instruct them with the commands. Very few delve into the cause of the dogs' behavioral problems. This is the reason why so many dogs revert after their training.

He was right. Some of my consultations with dog owners made me question myself. Why am I hassling a mind that is closed like a steel trap? It seems as soon as mental pressure forces it open, its springs close again, catching in it my fingers of involvement.

"The name change is more for the owner than for the dog. It is for the emotional connotation it creates in the owner. For instance, what would you feel if Princess were now called Susie?"

"I would not like that at all. I cannot feel anything, when I think

70

of Princess as Susie. It doesn't fit her."

"Let me demonstrate something: Susie, Susie, Susie! Did you get any feelings when I was saying it?"

"No, it left me cold."

"Great, now listen to this: Princess, Princess, Princess!"

"Mmm, I sure love her name, it sounds like music to my ears. It really fits her, my royal princess. But I do not see what you mean. Susie turns me off, Princess turns me on!"

I mistook the serious look on his face as conceding to the name change.

"I know now! All I will have to do is say her name Princess in a rough tone of voice. That should convince her I mean business!"

"Have you tried that before?"

"Of course."

"Did it work?"

"No."

"What makes you think it will work now? You can choose any name you wish, for it's the emotional vibrations you project that need changing. It will then make it that much easier for her to accept the big change necessary in the relationship from servant to master. If you remain the same, so will she."

"I get the picture. It will be hard on me though! Can you take her now for training?"

"Sure, here's a contract to fill out while I put your Chesapeake in her new home."

"Can I say good-bye to her?"

"Let's say you already have." And with that I took her to her kennel run. "Please call me when you have chosen a new name." Mr. Trumbull just nodded as he departed.

The next morning at 7:00 sharp the telephone rang. "Good morning, Meisterfeld Ranch Kennels, may I help you?"

"This is Mr. Trumbull. I wanted to let you know that I cannot change Princess' name. It has bothered me all night long. I slept very little. No, I just cannot change her name."

Boy, what a way to start a day. I could not see myself jumping back into that boiling pot of kidneys. "You are right, Mr. Trumbull, I agree with you. Let Princess remain Princess. What time do you want to pick her up? No, I will not charge you for her one night stand. Your deposit will be returned to you, too."

71

I am sure we both found his second departure (this time with his royal Princess) much more acceptable. As for Princess, I am sure she will live royally ever after.

Only receptive dog owners who are seriously willing to change their mode of interrelation with their dog—in order to eliminate the problem-causing stimuli—can be helped. Their reprogrammed dog will be able to maintain the newly acquired positive behavior.

A further analytical clue toward the nature of the problem can be revealed by observing the dog and his owner upon arrival for psychological testing—how they relate to each other.

Prior to testing I request a written case history. Each dog owner explains his personal experiences with the dog describing the dog's behavior in detail from the beginning.

Based on the summary of these components and the general idea of the behavior problem, the dog is put through a series of special tests, in the absence of the owner(s).

Although dogs cannot verbalize their thoughts and feelings in human language, they do reveal their mental and emotional states through their behavior, body language, and eyes, when they are tested in this respect.

Such specific tests evaluate significant factors like: adaptability, territorial boundaries, discrimination, attention span, sensitivity, tolerance, response to strange objects and noise, will-to-power, willingness to work, emotional dependency and demand, memory retention, fear level, etc.

During the subsequent consultation with the owner(s), we discuss their family relationships, their general philosophy and their standards. The dog training and corrective methods as well as the individual case histories are reviewed.

Now the "personality profile" and the overall picture is complete and the results can be presented by arriving at the cause of the problem. The necessary changes are outlined and the course of action is recommended.

I always point out to my clients the relevance of the saying "You get back what you give out" in your relationship with your dog, but you have to understand your interaction with your pet to its full extent. As in any relationship, the specific behavior of one partner inevitably influences the behavior of the other. The very sensitive organism called dog is no exception to this rule.

However, some owners cannot understand why their dog starts to misbehave or becomes vicious. They are convinced they have not done anything to harm their pet. They have bestowed only the best care and all their love on the animal. It is not quite as simple as that. A dog is much more sensitive to his environment than we usually are aware. Dogs pick up many details about us in daily life when we are relating to them. At every instant, they receive a flood of information about us by watching our body language, by listening to the changing nuances of our voice, by registering our different body smells (due to the physiological changes in the body chemistry) and then they respond.

We subconsciously communicate to them our emotions, our health condition, our state of mind, and problems in particular and general. When we are under stress, have health, marital or other personal problems, we project them to our dog, whether we are aware of it or not. The dog cannot help but be affected by all of these events, transmitted by subtle or obvious changes in our behavior. The more insecure a dog in the relationship with his owner, the more sensitive his reaction to any change. When the owner experiences a lot of problems himself, the ill effects on the animal will be stronger. The dog can exhibit health problems or behavior problems as an echo effect. However, the majority of people do not recognize this connection or do not want to be aware of it.

From the behavior problems of the dogs I have tested so far, I have always been able to draw conclusions as to the personal makeup and problems of the owners, as to their relationship with their pets. Their dogs were perfect mirror reflections of their personalities.

The conscientious dog owner truly interested in the welfare and salvation of his disturbed pet will either undertake the necessary steps himself to accomplish the inevitable changes regarding the behavior of his dog, or in the case of serious behavior problems, leave the dog for reprogramming with me. Though I have instructed some owners whose dogs had really serious behavior problems, on how to successfully reprogram their pets and themselves.

Mr. Allan Drucker of San Francisco was one of my clients who accomplished this task on his own with his Cocker Spaniel, Max. This is his story.

Max

By Allan Drucker

Max came to us as a four-month old puppy. Over the years he had caused us quite some trouble. Unfortunately, we had never taken the time to train him. When he was about 10 years of age, Max was affected by a lot of health problems, such as allergies, epilepsy, and a heart murmur. However, his behavioral problems were much worse, and so troublesome that they had become completely intolerable.

Max was very independent and possessive, and he guarded things. Nothing within his reach that he could carry was safe from him. He not only hid things, but also chewed them up so that they were hardly recognizable. We were constantly searching for kitchen utensils and personal belongings, which were beyond recovery when we found them.

Max was not friendly at all toward strangers, jumped at them and mounted them. He was really an antisocial dog. Persons in uniform were his primary target. He identified postal carriers with absolute certainty and made them his prey. We had to pick up our mail at the post office, because no carrier would come near our property anymore. We had already received several warnings from the post office before they eventually stopped delivery of our mail.

Max seldom obeyed commands. He did only what he wanted to do. He growled at us when we took something away from him, and several times even bit us. But afterwards he licked our hands with great affection, as if nothing had happened. A real Dr. Jekyll and Mr. Hyde.

The expert advice we received was to put Max to sleep. With all the problems he exhibited, there was no chance for salvation. But we were not able to accept that verdict. We were really very desperate when we came to see C.W. Meisterfeld as our last resort. Because my wife was six months pregnant, we knew we could never have Max around the house with an infant and would have to give him up. This was our last effort and only chance to save Max and be able to keep him after the baby was born.

Bill Meisterfeld gave us detailed instructions and suggested that we work with Max daily at home, which I did for an eight-week period, four times a day, according to the prescribed methods of psychological training. After that time, absolutely unbelievable for experts, Max became a completely different dog—obedient, social, always friendly, and trustworthy.

I continued my special training program with him for four more months. I was then able to take him to work and to any location where he met strangers and persons in uniform all the time. Everybody admires my well-behaved pet. Max enjoys playing with the baby and is completely reliable and loving. It is really a miracle. My only regret is that I did not use the psychological training concepts with Max 10 years ago.

SUMMARY
1. As dogs cannot verbalize their thoughts and feelings, the Freudian method of psychoanalysis is not applicable to them.
2. Their mental and emotional states can be analyzed by observing their behavioral responses and body language in relation to certain tests and stimuli.
3. The detailed written case history of the dog owners, their relationship with the dog, and their philosophy are an additional, valuable source for a comprehensive analysis and evaluation of the dog's problem.
4. Should you experience behavior problems with your dog, take the time to find out the underlying reasons before taking any course of action.

Detailed Evaluation of Doc's Case

Let us apply the fundamentals of the previous sections and analyze and evaluate Doc's case.

When Doc was chosen by his owners among his litter mates he was a very promising puppy. He was physically robust—the biggest and healthiest one of the litter, a leader from the beginning with a high will-to-power. Also, he was a very friendly and trusting puppy immediately approaching people who were strangers.

From the beginning, he was treated affectionately by his owners and fed the best. He received regular medical care from first-class veterinarians. He was happy to be with his owners, willing to please them, trusting and content. He even liked to travel with them in a crate. All the odds were in his favor. How and why did he become vicious and schizophrenic?

To his detriment, Doc was allowed great freedom. He did not receive any territorial and behavioral boundaries from his owners. House and field were his. Being given free rein to run reinforced his will-to-power and self-gratification, supported by his increasing adrenal reaction. When he wanted to, his owners played chew-biting with him, such as tug-of-war, and gave in to him in these rough games. Most of the time he was permitted to be the winner and to keep his "prey".

Sometimes he was yelled at and slapped, when he chewed on the wrong object. This he could not comprehend, because everything had the smell of his owners. The old socks and shoes they gave him to chew on smelled like the shoes, socks and sweaters they took away from him.

Another shock was his housebreaking. He couldn't understand why his buddies grabbed him by the scruff of the neck, rubbed his nose in the feces and tossed him out in the cold after he had performed a natural act for which they had praised him when on a walk.

He grew bigger and bigger, and his original high will-to-power increased simultaneously. Then, at the age of four months, he was chewing on his prey (a shoe) and his mistress tried to take it away from him. He defended it, and broke the skin on her hand, for which he was severely punished. In the past when he nipped on their hands and ankles, they had not only tolerated it but found it amusing. Here he crossed the line of respect.

The owners didn't recognize that the dog had reacted completely normally. They had conditioned him to chew and bite. They also did not consider the incident an alarm signal to change their interactions with the dog, but continued to advance in the wrong direction.

Doc was allowed to sit on the furniture like a member of the family. On the other hand, he was trained with methods of punishment and pain geared to break his will. Because they trusted and believed in traditional and published methods, Doc's owners used these recommended techniques on him, such as pressing his lips against his teeth, yanking his ears (Our late president L.B. Johnson was publicly castigated for lifting his two beagles by their ears on the White House lawn, but the experts still recommend it!), slamming him to the ground. Other methods such as flipping him over with a rope could have broken his spirit, if not his bones. He responded with fear and aggression.

During his first months with human beings he wanted a master, but was made to believe that he was their boss. Then the same human beings, who acted as subordinates, all of a sudden demanded obedience and punished him when he hesitated to obey their commands. They didn't understand that the treatment he received from them caused a conflict between his will-to-serve and will-to-power. Their catering had promoted his will-to-power and suppressed his will-to-serve, which declined further as a consequence of the force training.

When he was not in the field under training, he was made to feel in charge again by being spoiled and catered to. The poor dog could not understand this inconsistency at all, despite his high intelligence. He became very confused and fearful. He did not know what to expect at any given moment. His mind had not been structured in a consistent way establishing a system based on single standards.

Little by little he lost his trust in human beings completely and started to live on the verge of survival. He could not relax. His adrenals were triggered at the slightest and even most familiar incidents. He could never be certain about his safety. This fear and mistrust, coupled with too much affection and catering, were the main causes of his Dr. Jekyll and Mr. Hyde personality.

He began to feel especially vulnerable and cornered when in a crate, where he could hardly move and had no possibility for escape. He started to growl at human beings warning them that he was ready to defend himself when they approached the kennel and entered his immediate safety zone. The moment he was freed from his prison cell and had room to maneuver, he ceased his aggressive demeanor. He then had the choice of escape in case of a threatening situation.

The dog's next attack against his mistress took place in a walled yard without a chance for him to escape. He anticipated pain and felt cornered when she was going to put a collar back on him. The wide webbed collar must have looked to him like a switch in her hand when she approached him. Rather than waiting for her attack, his survival instinct took over and he attacked her first. How could he be expected not to defend himself?

When his master tried to force him into his crate he attacked him too, because he expected another punishment. It followed promptly. This time he was hit by an electric jolt.

The dog responded with another major attack in a situation he perceived as threatening, when his mistress worked on tick removal on his inner thigh (a very delicate spot being adjacent to the sensitive

77

belly area). A dog only uncovers this sensitive area when he is prepared to show complete submission. Doc saw no reason to be submissive; for him the opposite was true. He tried to protect himself and reacted instinctively and automatically to an imaginary dangerous happening on the spur of the moment. However, for this, his natural, self-protective reaction, he was punished again.

Despite all these adversities, the rest of the time Doc was loving and sweet to his owners, as his owners were to him. However, the dog did not trust them. And they could not trust him. Doc could not understand their complex human behavior. Being an animal, Mother Nature had not equipped him with the necessary reasoning to comprehend. What mattered to him was survival.

Unfortunately, his owners did not understand Doc's behavior and needs. They could not comply with them because of the overwhelming mass of misinformation. This is the reason that very promising dogs, like Doc, are being abused and made schizophrenic and vicious on a grand scale.

Fortunately, the majority of the canine victims of established negative training methods and their open-minded, loving owners can have a second chance through psychological reprogramming as preparation for a new and happy dog life.

SUMMARY

1. Doc's owners selected the puppy with the highest will-to-power. His great friendliness and trust toward strangers were even more important behavior traits.
2. Doc's owners wanted a family pet and a hunting companion with whom they could share life closely. To realize this goal, they followed their kind nature in everyday life with Doc and worked hard to train him with accepted methods.
3. The mixture of permissiveness and punishment directly contributed to the deterioration of his will-to-serve and promoted his will-to-power.
4. With this very harmful combination, failure was in store for them and their pet.
5. The dog lived on the verge of survival and was torn between his affection for and fear of his owners, which made him schizophrenic, a Dr. Jekyll and Mr. Hyde.

CHAPTER IV

CONDITIONING AND TRAINING

Conditioning in General

Now let us concentrate on the impact and methods of the conditioning and training we administer to our dogs when they come into our home environment. Conditioning and training can be accomplished either in an active or passive way, with positive or negative techniques. These have crucial consequences, leading to a happy or miserable fate for our pets.

The environment in which a dog is brought up has a major effect on his personality regardless of his heredity, and the conditions during the first six months have an especially potent influence. For instance, when we watch a litter of two-month old puppies, we see a variety of temperaments displayed—active, passive, timid puppies in all the different shades which form individual personalities. No two puppies will ever be alike. However, when we compare the characteristic behavior of these puppies with their later behavior as adult dogs, in many cases it will completely differ. I have often observed how a timid little puppy can become an aggressive full-grown dog; how an active, trusting puppy grew into a fearful, mistrusting, disobedient, vicious dog, due to the negative effects of his home environment.

All my clients with problem dogs confirmed the fact that their dogs behaved normally when they were small puppies. Without exception, these owners wanted obedient and socially well-behaved dogs. All these puppies were genetically sound and had the predisposition to grow into happy, contented, well-adjusted dogs giving the utmost pleasure to their owners. Unfortunately for them and for their owners, this did not materialize, because the dogs did not receive the conditioning they needed.

Even if we do not actively train our dogs, each time we relate to them we condition their behavior in a certain direction. Not only we, but also our dogs are creatures of habit. What we permit the cute puppy today is the conditioning for the adult dog of tomorrow. All the

Tug of War Develops . . .

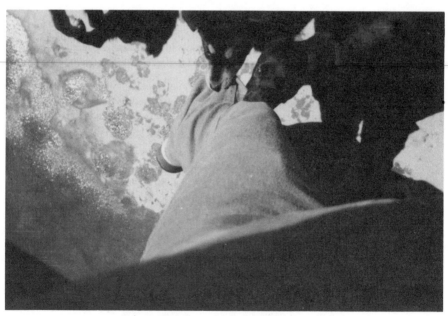

Into Pant Leg Biting and . . .?

Even Fighting Dogs Can Be Reprogramed

Without Punishment, Pain or Drugs – (See Chindo's Story)

Rage Syndrome

(See Toby's Story)

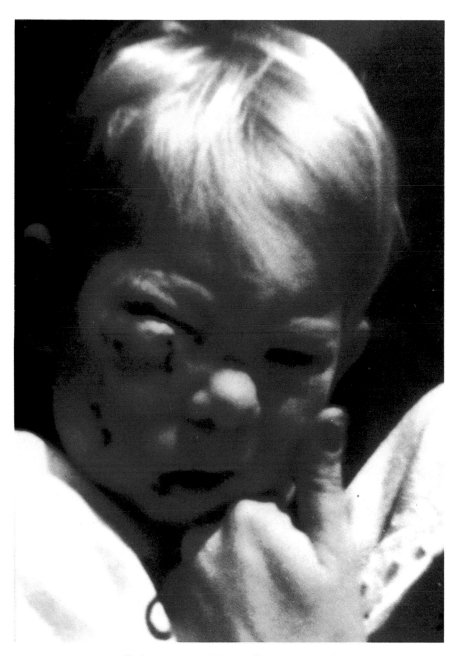

Children and Dogs Go Together!
Unfortunately, this child gave his dog *a hug and a kiss*.

Will To Serve

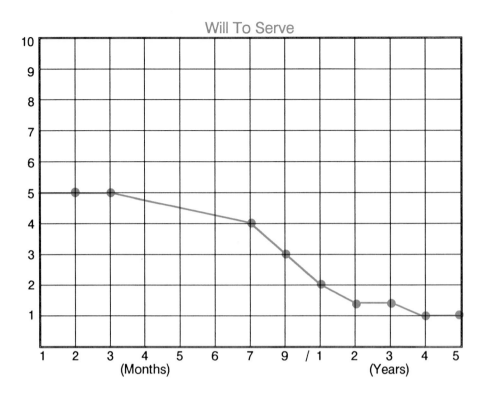

Will To Power

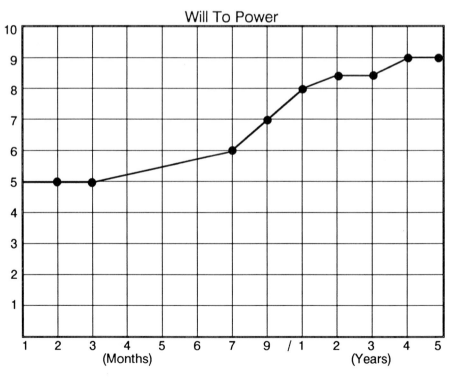

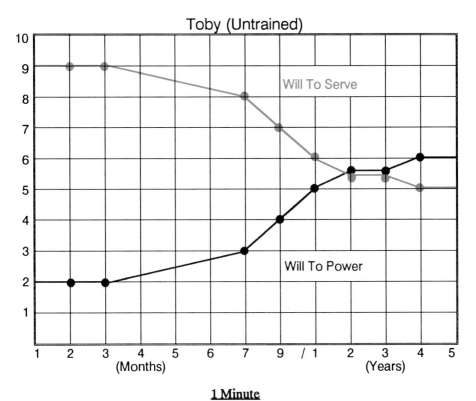

Toby (Untrained)

Will To Serve

Will To Power

(Months) / (Years)

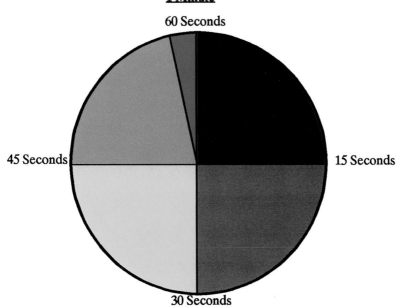

<u>1 Minute</u>

60 Seconds

45 Seconds

15 Seconds

30 Seconds

Discrimination Safety Period

Any Way You Look At It:

HE JUST WAS NOT KISSABLE!

Adrenals

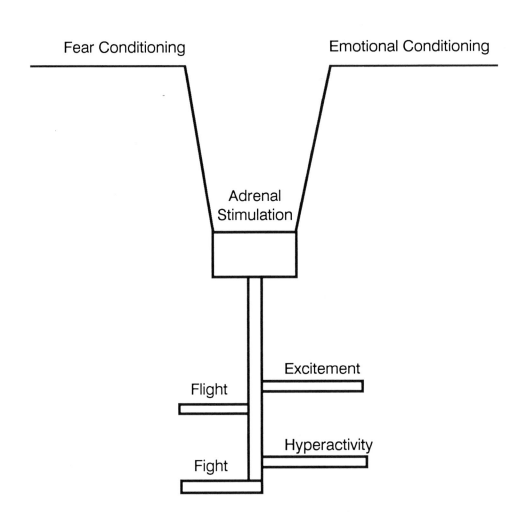

Disciplined Mind

Fear Conditioning

Emotional Conditioning

Adrenal
Stimulation

Excitement

Flight

Hyperactivity

Fight

Liverwurst Phase

Willingness To Retrieve And Deliver

Even a Meaty Bone

Temptation Ignored

Servitude Versus Bones

Jellybean Willingly Kennels...

...Into His Old Crate!

Acceptance and Trust

Friendly and Ready

Memory Relation Response (M.R.R.)

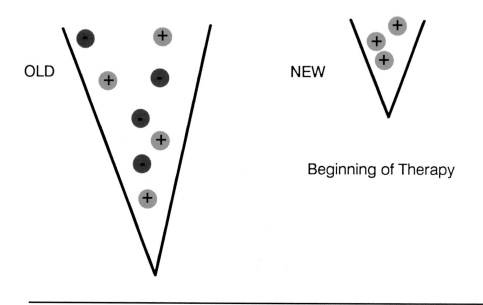

OLD

NEW

Beginning of Therapy

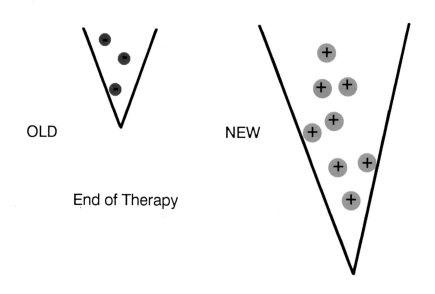

OLD

NEW

End of Therapy

Obedient

Acceptance and Trust

95

Wait a Time With Patience

Friends Reunited Going Home

happenings and experiences of the present will be integrated into the pup's behavior pattern of the future. That is one of the important facts of life that dog owners fail to realize. They cannot expect their pet to recognize and understand that a certain activity which is right one day might be wrong on another. Dog owners have to be aware that the dog's bad habits will get progressively worse with maturity. When they become unbearable, most owners see no other possibility than to take the pet to the Humane Society or S.P.C.A. Who is failing whom?

When the puppy in the litter tries to nip his mother or to do something else undesirable to her, he is put in his place right then and there. With motherly love, and at the same time the necessary firmness, she lets the pup know who is top dog in the omnipotent and omnipresent pecking order.

Now the puppy comes into the human family. Here is where Mr. Permissiveness starts his dangerous training course, dooming the pup's future. As your puppy is endowed with considerable charm, you find it mildly amusing when he growls and pounces about. And you really don't mind him sleeping on the furniture, sitting in your lap watching TV, or riding in the car. Will you still find it amusing and acceptable when the puppy has grown into an adult dog of 120 pounds or more?

How about the nipping puppy? It is you who lead him on the path from an occasional nipper to a fully fledged biter. It is as natural for a puppy to closely investigate everything in his new world with his nose and teeth as it is for a human baby to put objects into his mouth to evaluate them. When the puppy tugs on your pant legs or curtains, and chews on your old socks and slippers, you even admire him for these activities. How cute and adorable he is. You push him further onto the unlucky path by encouraging his increased usage of the teeth by buying all kinds of pretty chew-up toys, playing tug-of-war and roughhousing. He is even permitted to mouth and chew on your hand without scolding. He does not hurt at all, not yet...

The learning experience of placing his teeth on your skin is a symbolic act. The only difference between that and a pure bite that breaks skin is pressure. And then one day, when the puppy is not that little anymore, he gets carried away and does not notice how thin the skin is! This is called conditioning of a biter.

SUMMARY

1. Negative conditioning is present if the owner is not the necessary authority figure whom the dog can respect, and from whom he gets a sense of belonging.
2. Negative conditioning develops when the owner does not establish firm discipline and control, but is permissive with double standards.
3. Negative conditioning takes place if the owner does not train the dog at all, or not the proper way. The dog does not know how to please him.
4. A dog's mind is like rich soil; what you sow you will harvest. Vicious dogs are not born but made by their owners.

The Pavlov Principle

How can the behavior of our dogs be actively influenced and modified?

Ivan Pavlov, a famous Russian physiologist (1849-1936), proved that with careful programming and stimulation, a relatively permanent change in behavior (a conditioned response) can be attained. He discovered this in his classic experiment with a dog. By combining a signal with food, he found out that after a period of repetition he only needed to ring the bell, without presenting food, to have saliva flow freely.

In this series of trials the dog was conditioned at first to respond to two paired stimuli. The bell, the neutral stimulus, only alerted the dog at first. The food, the primary or unconditioned stimulus, was always followed by an unconditioned response, the excretion of saliva. Later the bell served as the sole stimulus and became a signal and substitute for the expected food, and was sufficient to trigger the saliva flow, an unconditioned response. The dog learned to associate the sound with food and to respond to the sound only.

In this process the bell became the trigger for the memory of the very pleasurable experience, food. Hence, every time the dog heard the bell ring, he looked forward to the food—a purely positive conditioning. This is is the same process applied in psychological dog training.

The bell or any other signal can be used as well to trigger the memory of a negative experience such as punishment, if both are collectively conditioned. In this case the familiar sound will trigger a surge of *adrenal* flow through the dog's body, instead of a saliva flow. That means the dog is alerted and prepared for an unpleasant, dangerous event. Then, when you get into his personal territory, the dog will either back up from you with fear, or attack you aggressively, as a consequence of a memory relationship response. (See MEMORY-RELATIONSHIP-RESPONSE, and chart on Page 94)

SUMMARY
1. The Pavlov principle is a very important key in dog training.
2. The memory recall of pleasant experiences connected with the positive methods of psychological training improves the cooperation of the dog and his learning progress.
3. When traditional training methods involving fear, punishment and pain are used, the memory recall of these negative experiences can make the dog more fearful and/or more aggressive, depending on the level of his will-to-power and survival instinct.

Negative Training Methods, Errors, and Dangers

Unfortunately, traditional, forceful methods are still dominating the field of dog training and are even offered under the guise of a new and positive approach, misleading millions of trusting and unsuspecting dog owners.

As a rule, the dog is forced to learn a certain behavior in order to avoid a disagreeable experience connected with discomfort, punishment and pain. The negative stimulus is used to terminate an unwanted behavior, or to induce a wanted behavior.

Any forceful training method, including pain avoidance methods, is based on fear, on breaking the will. Attacking the survival instinct, forceful methods can usually produce fast results. However, depending on the individual dog's assertiveness or will-to-power, supported by his survival instinct and his tolerance threshold for pain, the quality and quantity of punishment and pain application must be periodically adjusted. When the pain endurance level rises, the negative stimuli have to be increased simultaneously in order to maintain a certain behavior. If the negative reinforcers do not keep pace, the dog tends to revert. They also have to be applied consistently.

Feeble negative stimuli have only a temporary effect, lasting only until the dog gets used to them. He develops a sort of callus. A stronger dog in the physical and psychological sense needs a greater amount of painful stimuli and a longer, more frequent application period to condition him in a certain, desired way. In weaker individuals, feebler stimuli can usually produce the required effect in less time.

There are exceptions, when using a negative method is so effective that the owner does not need to reinforce it. The dog gets the message for that particular point. Yet, during my counseling practice with hundreds of dog owners over the past 25 years, I repeatedly found the negative approach to be ineffective, because the dogs were not mentally strong enough to tolerate the effects of punishment and pain. At a certain point, the dog's mental and physical tolerance limit is reached, and the dog flips. This mental breakdown can be triggered by various situations and events not directly connected with the act of training. For example, a certain noise or the innocent gesture of an unsuspecting person, perceived by the dog as threatening, can be the negative stimulus for the dog. Dogs who have been well behaved for several years become overtly disobedient, severely destructive, aggressive, and start to bite even their loving owners.

These dogs are then labeled "vicious". A more appropriate description would be "innocent victims" of cruel, inhumane, dangerous training methods practiced by millions of misled, unsuspecting dog owners and handlers. In the name of training, dogs are practically being tortured if they fail to obey. Punishment is never used for taming and conditioning wild animals in a circus, whereas with a reward system these animals can be successfully trained to obey man.

Why are punishment methods, which harm the object and are directed against the survival instinct, used on dogs (and even children) if they do not work with wild animals, whose behavior is predominantly ruled by stronger primitive instincts, especially survival?

In addition to the other faults, forceful methods burden the system of the dog with negative stress. Yelling at the dog or giving commands with a thunderous voice immediately produces a negative physiological effect on the dog's system.

When polygraphic equipment was first tested under controlled laboratory conditions, the dog was used as guinea pig because of his similar responses to certain stimuli, which can be correlated to those of humans. The heart rate rose, the pulse frequency increased.

REPRIMAND
With an Angry Tone of Voice

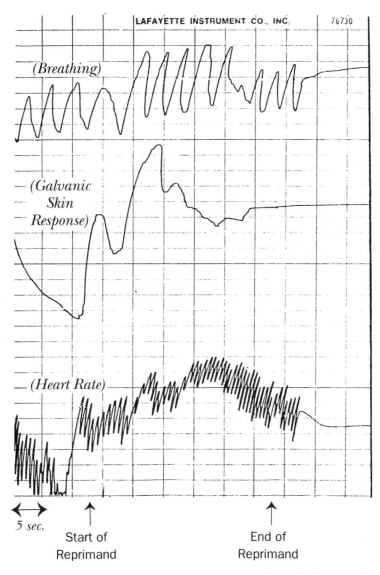

LAFAYETTE INSTRUMENT CO., INC. 76730

(Breathing)

(Galvanic Skin Response)

(Heart Rate)

5 sec.

Start of Reprimand

End of Reprimand

According to Leonard Saxe, a professor of psychology at Boston University and principal author of a 1983 study on polygraph validity for the Congressional Office of Technology Assessment, "The polygraph doesn't detect lies, it records such telltale signs of anxiety as increased pulse, breathing and perspiration."

NONVERBAL REPRIMAND
Finger Pointing

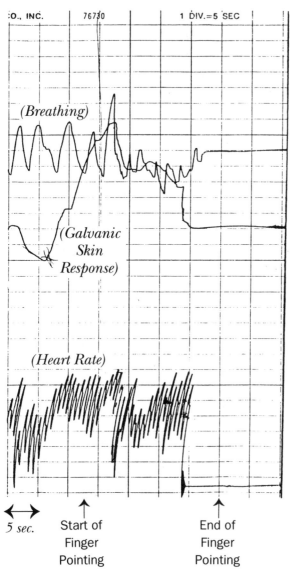

(Breathing)

(Galvanic Skin Response)

(Heart Rate)

5 sec. | Start of Finger Pointing | End of Finger Pointing

Considering the impact of nonverbal finger pointing at a person, it becomes obvious how much a dog is negatively affected by any threatening body gesture.

Dr. Albert Mehrabian, a noted researcher in the field of nonverbal communication (UCLA) found that only 7% of our feelings and attitudes are communicated with words, 38% via tone of voice and 55% through nonverbal expressions.

POSITIVE CORRECTION
With a Soft Tone of Voice

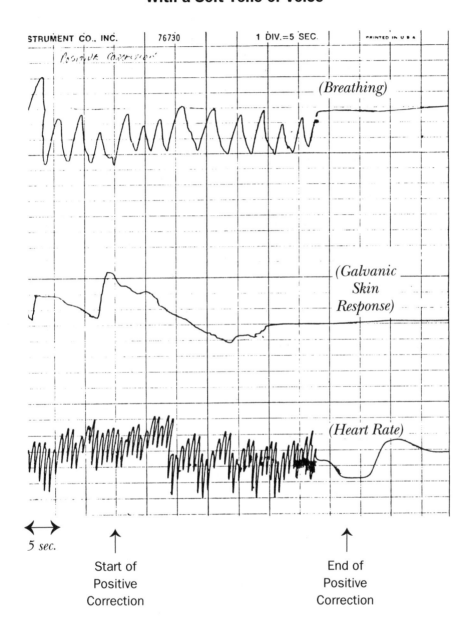

In a parallel vein, I have run polygraphic experiments in a management seminar for humans entitled *Mutual Respect Behavior Management* (from which a video production was also created). We found that even though the subjects knew it was an experiment when the "manager" yelled or pointed his finger at the "employee," a real flight-fear response was registered on the polygraph. When a positive correction of behavior was suggested, the cardiac reaction was neutral and the "employee" was more responsive.

Which method would you prefer to be used on you?

a) The Angry Reprimand/Finger Pointing, or
b) The Positive Correction of Mutual Respect (with a soft tone of voice)

I am at a loss to understand why dog authorities still consider and recommend punishment, pain, and other negative methods as a better way to train a dog than using positive reinforcement. I can only assume that negative methods are favored by our instant society because they lead to fast results, are completely unsophisticated, and do not demand any real understanding of dog behavior. In addition, in some cases they can possibly be an outlet for accumulated personal aggression and are an expression of insensitivity toward the dog regarding his needs and feelings.

Now let us scrutinize the most famous of these methods and how they are camouflaged to prove their usefulness to the dog owner.

HOW *NOT* TO BE YOUR DOG'S BEST FRIEND

Based on the "back to nature movement", the dog literature is full of "helpful" training instructions on how to teach an unruly pet obedience, assumedly derived from natural behavior of the wolf or the dog.

The chain is as strong as its weakest link.

Suppose you want to tie together two five-foot long chains of hardened, high-quality steel with one-inch-thick links. You connect them with a piece of string. How strong is this chain?

The chain is as strong as its weakest link, the string.

What does this have to do with the dog training literature?

Everything. The books written by authorities/trainers supposedly teaching "positive" dog training and reinforcement contain many valuable instructions and general ideas about training. However, when it comes to correction you are instructed to use force, punishment, and pain. You are led to believe that is what your dog needs and likes, even though his growls tell you to back off. Some of these instructions are downright dangerous and cruel.

This is the weak link. It is more important in determining the end result than all the good training procedures attached to it.

For this reason, my recommendation to the readers of all these great-sounding titles is to look for the weak link before you apply the recommended disciplinary techniques in the training of your pet.

It takes only one weak link in your training system to destroy the communication between you and your dog and also his innate trust and respect for you. This is what took place with Jellybean and Rambo (his story follows) and their owners.

The majority of dog books teach the following methods, which I have evaluated with a danger rating from 1 to 4 (1 highest risk, 2 moderate risk, 3 lower risk, 4 slight risk), in order to point out the possible hazards involved in their application. However, the lower rating could drastically jump to a higher rating with any given dog.

The Tone Scourge
Thunderous Commands

Give your commands with a thunderous voice. Yell at your dog, and let him know you are angry.

This is pure fear conditioning and does not establish respect at all.

How much respect do you have for a person who indulges in screaming at you?
DANGER RATING: 3

Shake/Throw Can

Startle your dog with a throw can when he is misbehaving and scare the hell out of him.

At one of my college seminars on canine psychology, I was demonstrating the shake can and taking the audience by surprise with this loud and rattling noise. The students could not tolerate it. Then I threw the can against the wall. A young lady jumped out of her chair in panic. The startling noise not only caused her discomfort but also triggered in her the memory of a painful experience she had had a few months earlier.

Her Golden Retriever was misbehaving in the living room. She threw the shake can close to the dog. It startled her dog so badly that his flight/fight mechanism (survival instinct) was activated and he jumped through a glass window.
DANGER RATING: 2

The Ear-Piercing Whistle

Blow a whistle as loud as you can—if possible into the dog's ear— to discipline him for unwanted behavior.

This is another distinct example of shock and fear conditioning.

Considering the dog's excellent hearing ability, which is much better than ours, he perceives loud and sudden noises, such as yelling, shouting, rattling, etc., as a threat triggering the fear/defense reflex in him. Blowing an earpiercing whistle into his extremely sensitive ears can drive a dog paranoid.

Loud, unexpected noises in general are not only disagreeable for a dog, but he associates them with negative events, such as danger and pain. The result can be either escape or aggression resulting in biting.

How do loud, startling noises and high-pitched whistles affect you?
DANGER RATING: 2

The Shock Collar

This so-called training device is widely applied in "modern" dog training on a "scientific" basis. According to the literature, you don't need to put on tennis shoes and chase your dog with a stick. You can do it with a remote-controlled, precisely calibrated electric shock device, the effect of which is adjustable from discomfort to pain. Dogs can be observed to flinch, tense, or yelp, when the jolts of different strength (up to six levels of intensity) hit them.

According to owners who previously used shock collars on their pets before they brought the dogs to me for rehabilitation, they had to increase the electrical "stimulation" to the highest level after a period of time, because the effect wore off. Furthermore, it did not correct the dogs' problems.

Once I had to reprogram a black Labrador and a Visla, which were used for pheasant hunting. Their owners had employed shock collars exclusively and extensively in their training for hunting with the result that the dogs would never leave the side of their owners. These very sensitive dogs had become completely insecure.

I personally witnessed other field trial trainers using shock collars in training. In some cases they showed the desired results immediately, whereas in others they could not stop the dogs from breaking on shot or chasing a flushed bird.

Although this device can be very effective for some dogs, highly sensitive and shy dogs with a low will-to-power can be ruined. Thus, it is very important to really know your dog's personality makeup before you even consider the use of an electric collar.

However, also in dogs with a high will-to-power and a lot of sensitivity, such as Jellybean and Rambo, the shock collar can compound the existing problems.

DANGER RATING: 4

The Hard Jerk

In this system the dog owner is instructed how to get an extra firm grip on the leash and how to pivot from the waist to ensure extra leverage to jerk the dog firmly when he makes a mistake. If the dog snarls and snaps, a repetition with an even harder jerk accompanied by a loud "NO" is recommended. If the dog attempts to or does bite again, the final suggestion is to seek the help of a professional trainer.

My comment: How absurd that a professional gives advice to the dog owner knowingly setting him up for a possible bite by his dog; then relieves himself from the responsibility of the negative consequences of his teaching method by recommending the help of a professional. (Who?)

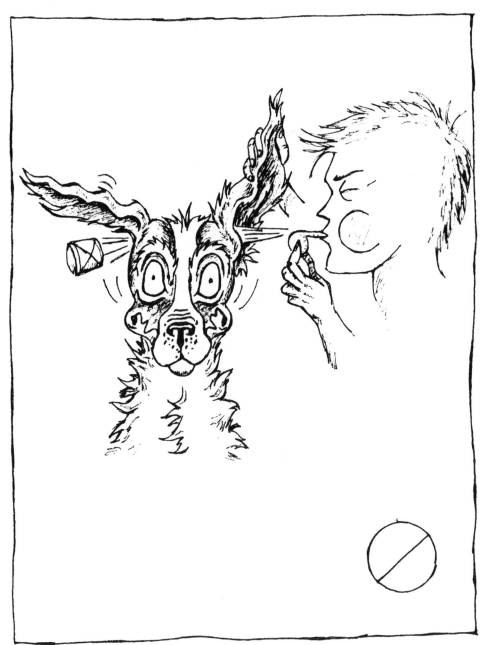

EAR PIERCING WHISTLE

A professional should not give any advice to a dog owner which makes a dog more aggressive.

DANGER RATING: 3

The Uppercut

Teach your dog discipline by hitting him under the chin. Be sure to hit the pet hard enough to get at least a yelp. Otherwise it will not be sufficient.

What does a yelp from your dog mean? There can be no doubt that this is an expression of pain and fear. I am sure the reader will agree that this cannot be considered a positive way of training.

DANGER RATING: 2

The Scruff Shake

Grasp your dog with both hands on his neck scruff and stare into his eyes. Then violently shake him from side to side scolding him in a low, loud tone with, "No." Even more effective is lifting your dog up in the air while staring, shouting, and shaking him, and then abruptly dropping him to the ground.

This method was "created" by observing the mother dog lifting up her immature pups with her mouth and slightly shaking them when they misbehaved. Obviously, it has not been considered that she does this only to the helpless, very young pups. When they are older, she keeps them in line just with an oral reprimand.

Be thankful that the instructions do not advise you to use this method to the full extent, by lifting up the dog with your teeth instead of your hands.

DANGER RATING: 2

The Field Trial Shake

The field trial version of the scruff shake is to lift the dog off the ground by his ears and, while vehemently shaking him, blow a whistle in his ears, instead of yelling at him, to really get the message through to him.

DANGER RATING: 1

The Stringing Up and Hanging

Another method being used and taught by trainers, especially in group obedience classes, is to string the dog up. This is used when a

CHIN SLAP

dog misbehaves or is disobedient, and when the other methods of heavy jerking, hitting under the chin and yelling do not lead to the desired results.

Dog owners are instructed to hold the chain short, lift the dog off the ground and hang him there until he is gasping for breath. They are supposed to drop the dog to the floor before he suffocates.

For highly aggressive dogs, one inhumane trainer even recommends pounding the obstinate pet in midair, striking him on the muzzle with a wood-reinforced rubber hose.

DANGER RATING: 2

The Flip

This training technique is recommended for dogs chasing cars, bicycles, joggers, children, etc. A 20 to 30 foot nylon cord is attached to the dog's collar. As soon as he reaches its end, while indulging in his chasing instinct, the handler runs in the opposite direction and the dog is flipped over. The cord length is increased to 40 or 50 yards for hunting dogs. (However, hunting dogs are now usually trained with the electronic collar.)

This flipping over can cause a torsion of the dog's stomach, i.e., the stomach twists in the abdomen. I have heard of a few incidents in which the owners practiced the flip on their dogs, but were not aware of the resulting torsion. The dogs died within a few hours.

DANGER RATING: No danger for the owner, but it has the potential of reducing the dog's life span to a few hours after application.

Alpha-Wolf Method
(Lift-Up/Roll-Over/Stare Method)

This training technique was derived from the behavior of wolves and is an incorrect interpretation of the method of the pack leader in maintaining the ranking order.

The enhanced "human" version consists of lifting up the dog by the scruff of his neck and throwing him on his back to the ground, holding him down and staring into his eyes.

This so-called alpha-wolf or alpha-dog method is an entirely imperfect copy of the genuine interaction of wild canines and even our domestic dogs. It completely overlooks the fact that every pack member knows his position within the group, and a weaker animal usually assumes a submissive posture "voluntarily," and the dominant one does not need to throw him on his back. Even in a ritualized dominance fight the loser gives in by submission without a further contest of wills.

When a dog owner (who is in no way respected by his dog as the leader) throws the pet on his back forcing him into a submissive position, fear and rebellion can be created in the animal. Unfortunately, man applies canine customs imperfectly and perverts them to enforce his leadership over his dog with the intention of conditioning and accustoming him to the human environment.

This method, used for establishing a system of rank and order between man and dog, is doomed to fail not only because it is wrongly applied, but also because the days of the wolf pack leader are numbered from the beginning. His position is only temporary and is jeopardized as soon as he drops his guard. An alpha wolf remains in his leader position only as long as he is physically strong and mentally alert enough to cope with his challenging subordinates. This guarantees that only the strongest and fittest is in the power position to insure the survival of the pack.

The behavior of canine superiors and inferiors is governed by inviolable rules originating from their hereditary patterns. In other words, there is a certain fixed and binding behavior associated with the ranking order. We human beings, accustomed to double standards and making compromises are not able to adhere to those strict canine rules. The dog will immediately notice our failure every time.

The most vulnerable position, which a dog assumes in response to a dominating adversary, is to "voluntarily" get down on his back and present his unprotected belly. He can be forced to do this only as long as he feels weaker than his rival. *He no longer will accept this* when he feels stronger than his adversary. The dog will use any opportunity to retaliate against his opponent and challenge him. This is one of the main reasons why many dog trainers, who teach puppy socialization classes, will not accept any dogs over six months old.

A dog, trained and made forcefully obedient by a human being with the alpha-wolf method, feels completely insecure and will attempt to subordinate his owner. From the dog's point of view the human has no real authority. The dog will promote himself to the leader rank as soon as he reaches maturity and feels strong enough. The dog can then cast off his obedience to his owner's commands learned as a puppy. The dog conditioned with this method revolts

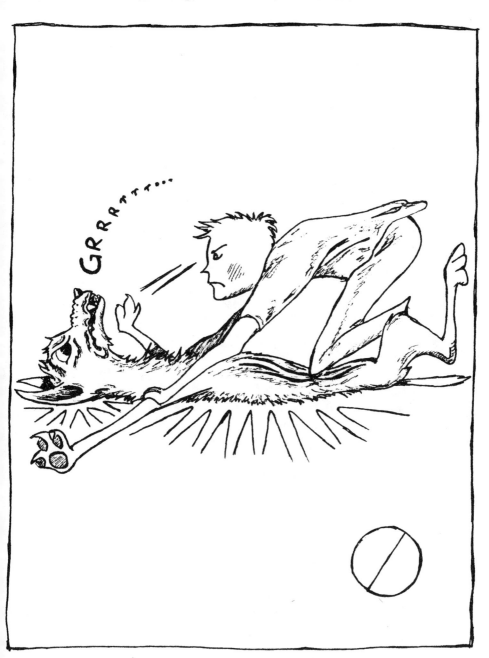

ALPHA WOLF ROLL

with unprovoked assaults on other animals, children, and adults and eventually his owner. He proves his new position as top dog.

When you engage in a battle of the wills, which is the essence of the alpha-wolf/alpha-dog and other forceful methods, the stronger individual aggressively dominates the weaker one. The dog has the best possible tools to eventually reach this goal—his teeth. An emotionally weaker dog trained with the alpha-wolf method becomes more and more intimidated. He will exhibit increasing shyness and fearfulness. His growing and overwhelming insecurity will result in the slightest incident triggering his self-preservation instinct, ending with a bite. It's a vicious cycle. As many examples prove, there is no doubt that this is a very dangerous method, especially with a full-grown, large dog.

Some authors/trainers mention the possible dangers of using the alpha wolf-method on highly aggressive, large and mature dogs, and recommend instead employing the services of a professional to "dominate" the rebellious pet. However, this method is not even "foolproof" when practiced by a trainer. During one of my seminars on psychological dog training, a student told in class about a demonstration of the alpha-wolf roll which she had witnessed.

A well-known and successful local trainer attempted to demonstrate a roll-over in a group-training class with an aggressive, three-year old Akita. To ensure the safety of the trainer, the dog was muzzled and had a cord tied around his face and head. During the "domination" struggle the tie around the dog's jaws came loose, the muzzle came off, and the trainer ended up with the battle scars of 39 suture marks in his face. Because of this incident, the Akita was condemned as unsalvageable, and the owners, who loved this dog very much, had to make the emotionally difficult decision to have the dog destroyed.

During the early seventies, a wolf-hybrid, a mixture of a pure bred timber wolf and a German shepherd, or a wolf/malamute mix, became very popular in California. These wolf-hybrids complemented the "free-spirit" movement of this period. The concept created a market value of $500-$1000 a pup. Since these hybrids were considered more wolf than domestic dog, they were trained with the alpha-wolf method. They were very tractable and learned the various obedience commands, but they exhibited a very unpleasant habit. When they were called with the "come" command, they all left a trail of urine behind them, regardless of whether they were male or female. The owners could not call them when in the house in order to protect their expensive carpeting from their soiling pets.

When some owners brought their animals to me for rehabilitation, I explained to them that it is a natural tendency for a dog to urinate when he is operating on fear induced by the domination-oriented alpha-wolf method, because this technique is based on fear/submission and not on respect and servitude, the fundamentals of psychological methods. Surprisingly enough, those wolf-hybrids, with a very strong wild genetic behavior, took to psychological reprogramming. Eventually, the "come" command did not trigger a fear/submissive behavior and the carpets became and remained safe from that time on.

The alpha-wolf training method destroys the confidence of shy dogs and conditions their fearfulness and panic reactions. It makes the strong-willed, aggressive dog more aggressive, increases resistance in a stubborn dog, and contributes to the nervousness and confusion of a hyper dog.

DANGER RATING: 1+

After serious study I find all these techniques distressing and revolting. The mentioned examples briefly describe what dog owners are advised to do by current authorities, and what our dogs have to endure. How can you, the dog owner, who want to train your pet to become well mannered, be expected to practice these negative techniques? How can you be sure the dog will not respond with fear or aggression at some time? Considering the repercussions, the statement "seek a professional if your dog continues to growl and bite" sounds like a bad and dangerous joke. The unfortunate consequence is that these professionals cannot save the animals who are the victims of their methods and then they recommend putting the dogs to sleep.

It is like encouraging parents to suppress and punish their unruly child, and when their methods compound the problem and make the child more aggressive, recommending a psychiatrist. If this does not bring a quick cure, which is not possible, then he must be confined.

Ernest F. Pecci, M.D., a noted California child psychiatrist and former juvenile delinquency expert for the California State Youth Authority, was often confronted with the fact that the environment of parental cruelty was one of the main reasons for severe behavioral disturbances leading to incarceration of adolescents. It is helpful to include

115

his comments on this subject because of the parallels between the results of child rearing methods and techniques for dog training.

"During the five years which I spent as chief psychiatrist in the Intensive Treatment Unit in Sacramento housing the most severely disturbed young criminals in the Youth Authority, I was able to see distinct patterns of antisocial behavior resulting from overstrict, overvehement, or inconsistent environmental conditioning. It frustrated the will-to-serve and exaggerated (in a distorted fashion) the will-to-power. Most of them had self-acquired behaviors which made them extremely egocentric and rebellious toward authority figures. Many exhibited instinctive reactions of anger and defiance to cover up fear, frustration, and confusion. All of them were lacking a stable sense of identity and had adopted various superficial roles to establish their uniqueness in the group.

"Often they would force the counselors to enforce an authoritarian role in order to test and to define their limits. The counselors who responded with punitive attempts to gain submission by breaking their wills with mace, shaking, or excessive confinement, only succeeded in arousing increasing reactionary defiance. Many of them behaved at times very much as do dogs to coercion and restriction.

" In every case, with the possible exception of a few young persons who suffered permanent brain damage from long-standing heavy use of street drugs, there was a consistent positive behavioral response to an approach of acceptance, mutual respect, clear and consistent expectations and praise for desired behavior.

"This is especially significant when we consider that many of these most severely disturbed incarcerated youths *were suspected of having a genetic predisposition* toward hyperactivity, learning problems, and compulsive acting-out behavior. Yet the *will-to-serve,* when properly activated, was found to be present in all of them."

How do you feel if somebody uses violence on you to force his will? Why should a dog tolerate methods which threaten his survival only because the trainer is or feels bigger and stronger?

The abused dog is even worse off than the abused child. The dog cannot express in words his feelings about what is being done to him. Unfortunately, he has no lobby behind him which condemns forceful training methods.

The story of Rambo shows what forceful training methods, including the famous alpha-wolf method can do to a dog's life, to that of his misinformed owners and to innocent bystanders.

Rambo

Rambo's owners got him from the Humane Society as a three-month-old Great Dane/Shepherd-mix puppy. Rambo was very bright, energetic, and affectionate, but he barked a lot. He was housetrained quickly, but he retreated into his crate when reprimanded. The owners started training classes with him when Rambo was about five months old. Altogether, they attended three classes and also worked with Rambo at home.

The training was done with intimidation techniques. In the beginning, Rambo was not very responsive to these forceful methods. Eventually he performed well, especially if he was rewarded with a treat.

When Rambo was about six months old, his owners purchased a dog book considered by a top animal behavior authority as a unique, major breakthrough in dog training. After reading it from cover to cover, they completely adopted the recommended methods. They made the dog sleep with them ("the alphas")in a "den" in their bedroom and used the recommended punishment methods on Rambo when he was ill behaved. The book made them true believers that the laws ruling the social interactions of the members of a wolf pack can be successfully imitated and applied to the relationship of man and dog.

When Rambo misbehaved, they corrected him with the "shake-down", with hitting him under the chin with the flat of their palm (later they had to use a closed fist, because Rambo would not yelp anymore), the "roll-over" into the submissive position with a knee on his chest, a loud oral reprimand, and the eye-stare. They also banished him for short periods. He was very slow to respond to these corrections and did not seem to be very impressed by the owners' disapproval.

Until the age of nine months the owners considered Rambo very affectionate and playful, and the"perfect" puppy, despite his barking fits and occasional spells of disobedience and aggression. Then he became more and more defiant in his behavior and there was less of the old well-behaved dog.

It became increasingly difficult to make Rambo follow commands.

SCRUFF SHAKE

They could only make him obey by forcing him. Rambo needed repeated corrections, one right after another. He became less and less eager to please. The owners received advice from professionals to stay firm, and that "this phase will pass."

Rambo had started to snarl and growl at the owner's wife while he was in advanced dog training, at about seven months. He was still small enough that she could feel in control and do the shake down.

In order to curb his aggressiveness they had him neutered at this age. However, they did not notice any reduction in his aggressive behavior. It slowly increased.

When Rambo grew bigger, the owner's wife became afraid to discipline him with the shake-down, and asked her husband, the dog's "alpha," to do it. From that time on Rambo never stopped challenging her when she punished him for a mistake. He would take verbal corrections and a long "down-stay", but he would challenge a hit under the chin with snarling and baring his teeth.

Rambo's overall behavior became more and more aggressive. He barked at and charged strangers, attacked and mauled the cats at home and in the garden, and chased trucks on the road if let off leash. He constantly barked if kept at home. Any sound on the road or in the garden would make him leap up and charge. Neither the electric dog collar nor any amount of other punishment could stop him.

This also applied to obeying commands. Rambo obeyed only if it was to his liking. The owners had no means to force him anymore.

On the other hand, the owners wondered why Rambo appeared to be frightened and seemed to feel threatened by loud noises, or when they carried a club-like object after they had punished him. They could not recognize the cause of his insecurity.

When Rambo was fully grown he started to challenge his "alpha" on correction. He would permit him only one sharp whack under the chin with his fist, but then bare his teeth and growl warningly. The owner became afraid to roll the big dog over on his back and to dominate him according to the book.

Then began a series of snaps and bites inflicted on people—children, visitors in the house, persons at other locations.

One evening Rambo's master took his bone away, because he felt disturbed by the noise. He gave him the "alpha stare" and tried to hit him under the chin. Rambo gave a warning bite on his hand and growled menacingly at him. That was the moment when Rambo had taken over completely.

Let us analyze why this sweet little puppy turned into a disobedient, aggressive macho dog.

When Rambo came to his owners, he had a will-to-power of about 4 and a will-to-serve of about 6. His will-to-serve was able to control his will-to-power in the early stages of training. Due to the fear and punishment training methods and the contrasting permissiveness of his owners, his will-to-serve was being turned off and destroyed; but his will-to-power grew with his age to the point of rebellion. Then the two wills clashed.

The law of survival became a predominant factor in the dog's behavior. His tolerance to accept the forceful training methods decreased day by day. The dog had signaled and warned the owners many times not to use punishment on him by expressing his unwillingness to follow commands, by challenging the owner's wife to prevent her from using the uppercut on him, and by expressing fearful behavior.

This case shows distinctively that there was no trust on either side of this owner/dog relationship. Unfortunately, Rambo's owner did not show enough sense of responsibility and consideration right from the start. He tolerated all these negative incidents, beginning with not taking action against his excessive barking as a puppy. He accepted Rambo charging his wife and himself when corrected, and even put up with his mauling cats, attacking, and biting people. Only when Rambo bit him and he became too frightened to handle the dog any more did he feel inclined to take action and put Rambo out of circulation. Rambo's owner was never really his master, but played instead the role of a permissive, inconsistent punisher.

What are the advantages of methods which work only in the beginning with the weak little puppy to force him into submissive behavior, but at the same time build up his instinctive fear of physical force and his resistance and rebellion against it?

There is no alternative to the principle that violence breeds violence in one way or the other. It is a primitive behavior pattern in animals and man, and has no benefits but only disadvantages. It attacks the strongest and most crucial instinct in all living beings—survival.

"The most violent form of fighting behavior is motivated by fear."
(Konrad Lorenz, 1953)

SUMMARY

1. Although forceful training (including avoidance methods) based on disagreeable, painful experiences seems to work with some dogs, punishment and pain in general is not a recommended means of structuring behavior.
2. Punishment is an unnecessary, aggressive, and primitive act in itself. It can lose its effectiveness within a certain time frame and can easily destroy the trust the dog naturally has for people.
3. The dog tends to associate people and training with displeasure.
4. Punishment attacks the survival instinct and can become an unconditioned stimulus for fear and breed resistance, defiance, hostility and open aggression. Rambo's story more than proves this point.
5. The development of fear in the dog cannot establish respect. It is a negative motivator for performance.

Psychological Training Methods
Based Entirely on Positive Reinforcement

In the process of training puppies and reprogramming problem dogs I use the Pavlov principle to establish permanent changes in their behavior. This learning experience is accomplished by means of reinforcement with positive stimuli. With this special stress-reducing presentation of information the rate of learning and remembering is increased. It guarantees that the training is a pleasurable experience and enhances the dog's self-confidence and trust toward his trainer. The dog is actually looking forward to his training sessions.

When I start a therapy/training program, I do not get involved with special problem areas of the dog. First, I create the *preconditions* for successful reprogramming, which is the solution to 85% of behavior problems. This consists of establishing a communication and **master-dog relationship based on mutual respect and trust.** From there I proceed to single out specific problems.

The routine begins with teaching the dog the basic commands of "heel/stand/sit/stay," and practicing them on a repetitious daily basis seven days a week for about two to three weeks, depending on the dog's problem. The duration of the single sessions is based on the dog's cooperation. When the dog has been trained with negative

121

methods, I may use new commands or whistle signals, in order not to trigger the memory of a frightful or painful experience in connection with the former commands used for negative conditioning (See Memory-Relationship-Response).

For example, if a dog is reluctant to follow a command, such as "come," it is possible that this command was originally conditioned with fear. In this case, the stay command should be taught first, and the dog should learn to hold for two to three minutes. Then it will be much easier to teach the "come" command. After six to eight weeks a recall of the dog with the "come" command can be done without negative consequences.

I teach the "come" command as part of a reward system at the end of my work sessions, after having my other basic training program reliably instilled for about two months. Especially with large breeds it is important, when the recall is taught, for the owner/handler to stand at a distance of five to six feet from the dog. The dog should receive the "come" command on a 6 foot leash, and be slightly pulled as an additional signal. After the oral command is given the owner steps backwards.

Special commands (one of these is the very important "leave it" command) are taught after the dog knows the other basic commands and has established trust and respect with the handler.

For this command I start with laying a bone on the training ring and walking up to it with the dog. When the dog tries to get to the bone, I say "leave it" and walk the other way giving a slight leash signal. When after some days of repetition the dog does not show any interest in the bone anymore, and turns his head the other way when we approach it, I use a praise system to reinforce his positive behavior.

If a dog has been unsuccessful in retrieving, because of force-retrieve methods, I will use a bone (sun-dried, bare of meat) for retrieve training. After the dog develops his willingness to retrieve (which is an extension of his willingness to work and please in his obedience training), I return to his refusal to retrieve a dummy or bird. If it's a bird, I first attach a few feathers to the bone, and gradually increase the size of the bone and number of feathers til the weight and size of the bird is reached.

During the continued process of disciplining (structuring and not punishing) the mind and reprogramming, I use a derivative of the Pavlov principle called "Unity-Praise-System." While Pavlov conditioned only two senses of the dog, his hearing and taste (See Pavlov Principle), I condition three. When the dog follows my commands in the desired way, I reinforce this with the positive stimuli **(1) Voice**, "Good Boy/Girl"; **(2) Touch**, a pat on the shoulder or chest area (pats are more related to a working relationship than stroking); and **(3) Tidbit**, such as liverwurst or cheese, so that he becomes eager to repeat this positive experience. It is important to observe the proper sequence in using these stimuli. The voice as the first stimulus has the strongest impression on the mind, then the touch should follow. The tidbit can be often omitted after some time and needs only to be given occasionally at variable intervals. This also applies to the other positive stimulus, the touch, which should not be overdone.

Some trainers feel that giving food during a training session is bribery, and that a dog will not perform without it. This may be true when you use it solely as such, because it will lose its effect after awhile. However, if you use it properly as an occasional reward together with and after the verbal praise and the pat, you psychologically condition your dog's senses of hearing, touch, and taste. Once these sensations are permanently instilled in the dog's subconscious mind, any time you use one of them, the dog relates to all three through association.

Another important point is that I never tire or overwork a dog in training. The sessions are always short and sweet. I quit training when the dog is still willing to please. Also, I always ensure that the dog reaches his full potential in training. Before I teach the dog any new command, I review the previous exercise and make sure that this level is solid. This is a guarantee that the dog does not become frustrated due to requirements impossible to meet. (My book, *Hows & Whys of Psychological Dog Training*, explains the teaching of basic and special commands in greater detail.)

Using this method, following commands becomes an overall positive and pleasurable experience for the dog and not a negatively enforced duty or contest of wills. Thus, his newly acquired behavior can be permanently and reliably instilled. It is the agreeable repetition that conditions the subconscious mind in the best possible and most reliable way.

There can be no doubt that the use of positive psychological methods is a better way to successfully shape the behavior of dogs and humans. This is confirmed by Dr. E.F. Pecci's kind endorsement:

"As a child psychiatrist, I have been interested for many years in C.W. Meisterfeld's work with behaviorally disturbed dogs. I recognize the relevance of his emphasis upon environmental conditioning of dogs to child rearing practices in the home. I have used many of his principles regarding the establishment of communication and mutual respect in my work with delinquent adolescents in the California Youth Authority with consistent success."

SUMMARY

1. The basic principle of successful training is to establish an atmosphere of clear communication, mutual respect, reliability, and trust from the beginning, and pair it with positive reinforcement.
2. This means clearly defined physical and psychological limits, so the dog can feel secure and confident.
3. Any disobedient behavior can be stopped at the outset with constant, firm insistence on proper behavior.
4. This will contribute to the owner's position of being respected and loved by the dog, without any power struggle.
5. A dog trained in this way will not break the skin of a person. He will extend his respect for the owner to other people.
6. You can catch more flies with honey than you can with vinegar.

CHAPTER V
A NEW BEGINNING

The End of Doc and the Delivery of Jellybean

Doc had no choice other than to share my company for the next few months. His owners had decided to leave him with me for reprogramming and eliminating his serious problems.

When I observed Doc after I put him in his kennel, these thoughts ran through my mind: What a dog! What an extraordinary sense of discrimination! He scans his surroundings within a fraction of a second. And how dangerous he is! I can't approach him closely. He growls at me and would bite if I invaded his personal "safety zone." He is so full of fear he doesn't trust anyone (See photos, Pages 86, 87).

It will take a lot of hard work and some time to break through to the roots of his fear—to extinguish and eradicate all traces of Doc's adverse behavior patterns which are so deeply ingrained in his mind due to the long-term negative conditioning. In the process of Doc's reprogramming and learning, these old "channels" will have to be abandoned and new neural pathways must be developed. The new behavior patterns will have to be permanently reinforced right from the beginning over a definite period of time to become instilled very strongly, and so be able to replace the old patterns (See chart on Memory-Relationship-Response, Page 94).

I did not lose any time. I immediately dissociated Doc from any negative conditions or situations which had the slightest potential to trigger the old adverse behavior patterns.

The first step in this direction was to give him a new name. "Doc" became "Jellybean." This new name did not have the verbal whipping power of the old name; even Simon Legree couldn't say "Jellybean" in anger. It became the symbol for *only positive* experiences in relationship to man, excluding all fear reactions. As the new positive behavior patterns are instilled in his mind without any pain and punishment, but with positive reinforcement only, his fear will not be supported and thus can subside and disappear.

Obviously, the kennel was a location Jellybean associated with a lot of fear. Therefore, I concentrated my efforts on this object. From the beginning I approached Jellybean's kennel run in a new, ritualized manner to win his trust and to desensitize and detach him from the fear association:

Man -> Kennel Run/Trap -> Pain.

Before he could see me from his run, he heard my bobwhite whistle, then I came into his vision by approaching his run in a non-threatening manner, calling his name "Jellybean" with a soft, gentle voice. I did not stare at him or respond to his menacing growling at me at all. I ignored it completely, dropped a piece of liverwurst into his run, and then left him alone. I repeated this procedure every 15 to 20 minutes throughout the day.

Unfortunately, in all the training books that I have read, the dog owner is advised to suppress the aggressiveness of his dog by an attack procedure. "Let him know who is the boss and top dog in the family." It is not even considered that the problem may have been created by the owner or others with an attack approach in the first place.

After four days Jellybean stopped growling completely. He found out that I was not a real threat when I approached him. He only heard the whistle and his name reinforced with liverwurst. My approach to his kennel became a pleasant positive experience for him. Jellybean started to be more relaxed and friendly. His growing positive feeling for me gradually eradicated his aggressive demeanor. Neither animal nor human can have two feelings at the same time toward the same object. Doc's fear/aggression response to man's approach, which his owner noticed every time he came to his run (Doc first retreated to the far end of the kennel or into his dog house), was now being replaced with a positive, friendly response. Making use of the Pavlov principle through a chain of positive associations, a new response was conditioned in his mind and a new neural pathway was shaped.

After building a foundation for our relationship of mutual respect, Jellybean was ready for his working sessions. When I began training, I constantly reinforced his new, positive behavior every four to five seconds with the bobwhite whistle and his name, but no food. Otherwise the tendency of the mind to relate to its old conditioning would have had a better chance to surface again.

Under no circumstances did I force Jellybean to go back into his small, personal crate. I did not want to reinforce his old fear. Also, I did not pressure him with other commands too soon. I had him on a long leash in the training ring, walked around and slowly pulled him closer and closer. If he had a tendency to lead, I would just stop, turn around and walk the other way talking to him, "We are going this way now." I had a conversation with him without getting into the "heel" command, in case "heel" had a negative connotation for him. When he refused to cooperate, I stopped the training completely and put him back into his big run. The important and critical point was not to trigger and reinforce his old memory-relationship-response of punishment. I did not put stress on him, and thus prevented training from becoming an unpleasamt affair.

As every living being needs love and attention, Jellybean found out he could get it by cooperating with me in the training process. As a result, after two weeks he was eagerly and affectionately waiting for me in his kennel. He was looking forward to his training sessions with me, and started to show eager-to-please responses to every command.

I continued reinforcing his positive behavior in the training ring with the Unity-Praise stimuli Voice, Touch, Tidbit (*Hows & Whys...*) for the next three weeks, and at the same time taught him his basic obedience commands: heel, stand-stay, sit-stay, and down-stay, both verbally and with hand signals. Jellybean fully supported my analysis of his intelligence and learning ability. Sometimes I had the impression this dog thought things out. His memory retention was far beyond the average dog's capacity. I have experienced only two comparable dogs. One was my obedience and retriever champion Baroness, a German Shorthair Pointer, and the other was Patches, a female Brittany Spaniel.

After four weeks, I began the next phase. Walking up to his run without the reinforcing stimuli (bobwhite whistle, liverwurst, voice), I stared at him with glaring eyes. This before had provoked his aggressiveness. Now I was intentionally triggering his memory of yesterday. In the beginning, I would not stare longer than five to eight seconds. I could see in his eyes some confusion, just as though he was trying to figure out what that meant, because before all my approaches had been preceded and reinforced with sound and taste. Now there was nothing but challenge. This stirred the fine line between his old and new behaviors—fear and trust. Before the old Doc could reappear, Jellybean was again reinforced with the three familiar stimuli. I repeated this every time I went to his run for a training session: Old fear trigger of Doc versus reward for Jellybean's pleasant behavior. Within a week Jellybean would not fall for my tricks any more. He would just sit there with his tail wagging, playing along with my game, patiently waiting for his treat.

We were now on the first level of mutual respect and trust, and could proceed to the next. I walked him into his run and slammed his kennel door behind me. With the slide to the inside run closed, he had no place to run, and I just stood there. After five to ten seconds, I put the three reinforcers into play. It took Jellybean only two experiences before it became another "try to trick me" game. I was starting to wonder if he hadn't already read about my positive reinforcement concepts! Well, he must have, because when we went to the next step, triggering his fear/aggression memory by putting him in his small crate and shutting the door, he just sat inside giving me that look of "when you're all through playing, don't forget to give me my liverwurst." After two days I was able to slam the crate door hard, and he had the patience of a saint waiting for his goodie. This positive development continued in every respect. Jellybean's growing trust in me (paired with the liverwurst treat) made his resistance and fear melt like a patch of snow in the spring sun. The crate became a place of pleasure.

When I took him to the veterinarian after eight weeks of training for his necessary innoculations, he coped well with this stressful situation. The veterinarian was surprised when Jellybean's past history was fully explained. This proved Jellybean was ready to transfer his positive responses to other human beings. He had learned he did not need to be afraid of them, but could trust and respect them exactly as he had when he was ten weeks old.

SUMMARY

1. Jellybean and I established a relationship of mutual respect and trust which became the basis for further successful reprogramming.
2. Through a conditioning process using only positive reinforcement, Jellybean gradually overcame his fear-aggressive behavior.
3. Jellybean once again became the friendly and affectionate pet his owners had originally hoped for.

Revelations
By Dick Flinn

When we left Doc at Bill's for reprogramming, we agreed not to call for eight weeks. Therefore, I was overjoyed when Bill called me after four weeks about a radio interview he was giving, and then at the end of our talk humanely added, "Jellybean is doing just fine and will see you on schedule."

Eventually, after eight weeks, the appointment day arrived. Bill demonstrated to us what he had accomplished with Jellybean so far, which was amazing. Also our friends, who were visiting from Michigan, could not believe their eyes. After that, three days of discussion and introduction to obedience-handling methods were scheduled.

I had two radically different types of thoughts. On the one hand I had always considered obedience maneuvers as kid stuff compared to the wide open performance needed at field trials. On the other hand, I felt genuine fear as to whether Jellybean would really obey me or revert to savage behavior.

As we talked prior to going into the elegant enclosed training ring I asked what I was to do. Bill said, "I'll tell you everything at the proper time." This scared me even more, but now I realize that the complexity of the workout depended on the success of the first few steps. The first order was to "take the end of the leash in your right hand and then grasp it with the left so as to leave slack between your left hand and the collar. Start out by *saying* "heel," then walk at a modest pace. Don't scold or punish the dog in any way and if he jumps up, continue walking."

I took the leash as told, promptly forgot to say "heel," and started walking. Jellybean exploded joyfully at my side, trying to lick at least my shoulder. However, I followed orders and gave a belated "heel" command. After ten yards Jellybean miraculously subsided to a walk at my side—and on a *loose* leash for the first time in my experience. Right then I had to admit there might be something to this obedience stuff. Then Bill said "Halt," I stopped, and Jellybean sat immobile! Next Bill said, "Tell him to stay, then raise your left hand, put the leash down and walk away." It worked like magic! Again I was told to pick up the leash first with my right hand, then my left, then walk. This time I remembered to say "heel."

Following this, we did the "stand" and "down" commands. We

noticed on the "down" command that Jellybean would sometimes merely stay in the "sit" position. Later Bill explained that the "down" command put the dog in the most vulnerable position and demanded a strong will to please. Even more important was that Jellybean did not fear me. I became happier and happier with the results, but Jellybean became less and less compliant and more excited. Bill ended the session on a good note, giving me some liverwurst balls for Jellybean. The second and third days also went well.

On the fourth day we came to take Jellybean home. Then tragedy struck. Jellybean's small crate was in the center of the training ring. After going through the usual routine, Bill said quietly: "Tell him to kennel up and shut the gate." I should not have been worried, because I had seen Bill do this several times without incident. But I was scared. Jellybean must have read my mind. He went in all right, but when I closed the door he growled and snapped. Only with difficulty did I close the latch. It was clearly time for a conference instead of a homecoming!

At this point Bill probed further into the past asking *if at any time* I had gone into his kennel or run to punish him. I had forgotten that one time my wife and a friend approached his run and he growled menacingly. They called me, and I decided it was important to be firm. Every book I have read advised "Don't let him get away with bad behavior. Let him know who is top dog in your family." I opened the run and Doc promptly fled into his dog house, where I punished him several times. I had just about forgotten this experience and only remembered it when my wife recalled it.

Bill said this explained the dog's aggressiveness regarding his places of safety, the kennel and the crate. Jellybean's homecoming had to be postponed because it was necessary to reprogram him even more deeply.

Relapse and Recovery

The principal reason for having Jellybean and his owner attend private training sessions at my center while the dog was still kenneled there was to enable them to meet each other on neutral territory, and to build their new relationship of mutual respect without fear on either side. The joint aspect was vital, because if one expressed fear, this would automatically trigger the same reaction in the other, a memory-relationship-response (See Memory-Relationship-Response). The understanding of this mechanism is very important to dog owners who desire to change their dog's behavior, especially if punishment and pain were part of the training, as in the case of Jellybean.

Sounds, scents, and visual impressions of a positive or negative nature are stored in the memory bank of the dog. When you tell your pet to sit and the conditioning stimulus was not based on punishment and pain, the dog will sit without his fear and instinctive survival response coming into play. However, when a dog is told to kennel or go into his crate, and is punished during or after this process, this is stored in his mind as a fear experience. Whenever he receives this command from the same person or others, he will be on alert. His survival is being triggered and he will respond accordingly.

That is exactly what happened when Jellybean's owner locked Jellybean's crate on the day scheduled for his homecoming. The problem was that despite the harmonious training sessions, the owner was unable to dispel completely his feeling of fear in shutting the crate door. His past experience with "Doc" was suddenly revived. This was sensed by Jellybean, and the dog's own memory of past incidents was triggered, too. He responded immediately with a growl. This is a graphic illustration of rapid sense perception and memory recall. The effect of this fear-to-fear encounter lasted long after the owner left.

After learning from Jellybean's owner about punishing the dog in the kennel, it took me four more weeks to eradicate this traumatic experience from Jellybean's mind.

Eventually, Jellybean was ready for his new relationship with his owners. Were they ready too? They would have to destroy the old profile they presented to the dog and step into new shoes and become the new masters. In their new roles, they would have to convince Jellybean that they also believed in mutual respect. Time would tell whether they were up to it. Certainly Jellybean was ready.

The owners were equipped with the necessary information to continue what I had started. They would need to strictly adhere to my methods of psychological training for a few more months in order to maintain the favorable conditions for his positive behavior until the new message was indelibly inscribed in his mind. Of course, Jellybean would have to have some patience with them, until they understood fully what he had learned. Now it was time for the other end of the leash to be taught new tricks. The stage was set for the new beginning.

SUMMARY

1. The extent of the dog's negative conditioning and relating to certain stimuli of the past, be it persons, places or things, must be known to the utmost detail *prior* to the rehabilitation process.
2. The final success of the reprogramming procedure depends on the change of the owners' relationship with their pet and their consistent relation to the dog in the new, proper way.

Witnesses II
by Paul and Barbara Trojan

When we heard from our friends in California about the progress in the rehabilitation of Doc (now Jellybean), we were delighted. We had an opportunity to visit Dick and Edwina and inquired whether we could see Jellybean in action. Bill Meisterfeld agreed, and we had the oportunity to observe Jellybean in action at the training center.

The changes were dramatic after eight weeks of reprogramming. All the aggression was gone. The dog we saw had the enthusiasm of the little puppy coupled with an attentive and eager compliance to a group of commands and exceptional control in retrieving. Jellybean heeled happily on a loose leash, dropped into the down position for Bill like a doormat, assumed the stay position without hesitation, and eyed his handler with a jovial look as if to say, "What would you like me to show these folks next?"

We knew the dog's reprogramming had been successful. Now it was up to Dick to fulfill his part as master and establish mutual respect and trust. We felt he was equal to the double task of avoiding permissiveness and punishment.

Jellybean's Homecoming
by Dick Flinn

After another four weeks I again rehearsed the training commands. Everything went smoothly. I felt secure now with my new pet, and Jellybean was obviously happy with his new owner.

We took Jellybean home in the back of the station wagon (no crate) without complaint.He also entered his new kennel run at home without displeasure, but with a new approach developed by Bill. I established Jellybean in a sit-stay position just inside the gate to the run without entering myself. I gave him a small cube of cheese with an "o.k." command and detached his leash. Then I quietly closed and locked the gate while Jellybean placidly walked around. The next morning it was a real pleasure to have him come happily to the gate instead of slinking into his kennel in fear.

After a few days, Bill visited to see how things were going. I was overjoyed to report the success in my attitude as much as in Jellybean's. I had been reprogrammed so that I no longer feared a menacing snarl and perhaps a severe dog bite. I accepted the fact that this was a new, reliable dog as long as *I* did not revert to the old patterns of permissiveness and punishment. It was an exhilarating feeling to walk our new Jellybean on a loose leash. Instead of having Jellybean tugging and looking ahead with a wild-eyed glaze for fields to be conquered, he turned his head happily toward me as if to ask, "where do *you* think we should go?"

A few weeks later my own conditioning was put to another severe and unexpected test. Bill called and said jovially he would like to take a few pictures of the new dog Jellybean. He didn't spell out the conditions! After some easy shots, such as "Obedient" (Page 95), he wanted another one. He showed me how, after giving the stand command, I should crouch to the dog's level and place my right hand under his mouth and my left under his tail. I gave the "stand" command and then, in a quavering voice, asked Bill if I should drop the leash, too. "Yes," was his answer. When I placed my hand under Jellybean's muzzle I had an evil flash pass through my mind for not more than a millisecond of the jaws turning and biting me. Before I could send out any bad vibes I looked at Jellybean's calm, respectful eye and slowly wagging tail and said mentally, "Be gone." (Acceptance and Trust, Page 95) I praised Jellybean as calmly as I could but with heartfelt appreciation.

Memory-Relationship Response

If Jellybean's owners had continued to relate to him the same way they did before the reprogramming, the dog would have had no choice other than to respond accordingly and to regress to his old responses. The old memories would be revived and override little by little the newly conditioned ones. The owners' inability to become masters of Jellybean would again force him to take over and exercise control over them. As his case history proves, this would again place him in an unwanted and frustrating role.

Even the greatest amount of love and affection extended toward him would not help to maintain Jellybean's new improved behavior. The only guarantee for maintaining Jellybean's positive responses was the owners' re-establishment of their natural and rightful position as his masters and their consistent interaction with him based on mutual respect and trust. The elimination of Jellybean's old detrimental memory patterns in relation to his owners was therefore a precondition for his new healthy behavior.

Have you ever thought of a traumatic experience in your life? It could have been six months, one year or many years ago. Stop reading for a minute and reflect...Did you notice how you were physically and emotionally responding?

The subconscious mind stores all experiences we have ever encountered in our lives, whether we remember them or not. When a special event is revived, triggered by a certain stimulus, our thoughts go back in time and space to when and where the incident took place. Body and mind reexperience the happening, just as if it took place that very day, regardless of whether the experience was pleasant or unpleasant.

To emphasize this point, let me cite a personal experience which has affected me for over 20 years. It was one that helped me understand my own behavior better, and why certain stimuli can recall a shocking and hurtful event even in a dog's mind.

It took place in 1951. I was drafted into the Army and stationed at Aberdeen Proving Grounds, Maryland. My attitude since my teens had been, "I can handle anything, at anytime, at anyplace." Of course, the 16 weeks of old army-style infantry base training we were going through were creating some doubts in my mind, but I was able to hold on to my old ideas.

One day a piece of my tooth broke off. I reported in, the captain took a look inside my mouth and, without further comment or suggestion of an anesthetic, he proceeded to drill.

No problem, especially not for me. I just started to get comfortable in the chair when it happened. My tooth was hollow and the drill went through it and right into my jawbone. Luckily, the captain's reaction was quick and he pulled the drill back immediately, because the only direction I could go was straight up. The pain was so excruciating that I refused to get back into the chair and walked out. Later in the morning I was ordered to report back to the dentist.

They spent a good half hour convincing me to let them take care of the Government's property, instead of waiting for furlough time to have a civilian dentist do the filling. I must admit this strange compassion they expressed for me was not what I had experienced up to that time in the army. After numbing my mouth, the job was finished. So was I, because for all these years I have been fighting that painful experience. Now the instant I sit in a dentist's chair my heart rate increases, and I break out in a cold sweat. I am sure the various dentists I have been to have seen it in my eyes—pure fear. Fear that happened only once and many years ago, but the memory-relationship-response was so strongly embedded that I relive it each time.

When a painful experience is set up to prevent a dog from doing something or after having made a mistake, a memory-relationship-response (See chart, Page 94) is conditioned in his mind. Each time the scenario is comparable to the crucial events of one or more traumatic experiences, this specific memory is triggered. The dog's response will be avoidance based on fear. The dog cannot help but relive the shock. This is particularly true for highly intelligent dogs, such as Jellybean, who are endowed with an exceptional memory. This is one of the reasons why I advise owners of problem dogs to change their dog's names to prevent a negative memory-relationship-response which could possibly be associated with a particular name. This is especially true if the owners have used it in a scolding voice or in connection with punishment (in almost all cases they have).

The development of a phobia as the result of a single dramatic experience can reach as far back as early puppyhood. A dog is unable to verbalize his deep-rooted fear and can only express his reaction in his behavior and try to cope with it in his own way.

Such was the case of Arnold.

Arnold

Because this was the first dog for either one of them, Paul and his wife Joan had been very thoughtful in getting prepared for their new puppy. Several weeks in advance, they discussed with the breeder how to be ready and what Arnold would need. They received good advice, from feeding him only in his dog dish and providing his own dog bed to house training. "Take him out first thing in the morning, frequently during the day and last thing in the evening to the same place, in order to teach him to use the back yard. Don't punish him if he has an accident in the house. Be patient and wait a while and he will learn." Every detail was covered to guarantee that everything would go smoothly when Arnold entered his new home.

The day for Arnold's homecoming arrived. Arnold was not fed or watered by the breeder that morning. He also was given an extra play-run exercise to prevent any emergencies en route. Paul and Joan were advised to cover the backseat (where Arnold was to ride home) with a blanket and newspapers to prevent any possible accidents. But these precautions were completely superfluous with Arnold and all went well on their drive home. Immediately after he had parked the car in the garage, Paul took Arnold to his pre-reserved "do your business" location in the back yard. Arnold complied promptly. Paul whistled and Arnold followed him obediently into the house.

Nobody could be more excited and happy than Paul and Joan with the smart puppy they had chosen and how well everything went. Joan picked Arnold up, just as she had been instructed to do by the breeder and carried him over to his dining area in the kitchen. Because it was a hot summer day, Joan thought, "First I will introduce Arnold to his new water dish. I'll bet he is dying of thirst." As she was going to put him down in front of his brand-new water dish, Arnold suddenly began wiggling and howling in terror, trying to escape. When Joan released him, Arnold ran away into the family room as if haunted by a thousand ghosts and decorated the carpet with a puddle.

Paul and Joan were baffled. Why was their new friend shaking and scared to death over a dog dish? That could not be true. "Did you pinch his skin when you were carrying him?" "Not at all," was Joan's reply. They went back to Arnold's dining place. "Maybe he is afraid of the location, feeling too squeezed into the corner." So they moved the dish more to the center of the kitchen. Joan got Arnold to follow her to this new spot by tempting him with some treats. When he was near the dish, he started to tremble again and ran back into the family room leaving another wet mark on the carpet.

Nope, it was not the corner. There must be another reason. Let's call the breeder. After listening to the past dramatic events for a couple of minutes, the breeder suggested that maybe the porcelain dish was too colorful. "We use just plain stainless steel dishes for our dogs." Off went Paul to purchase two new dishes, while Joan played with Arnold in the back yard. It did not take long and Paul returned with two shiny stainless steel dishes the exact make and size the breeder had told him.

They rushed back to the kitchen with a different plan of action. Instead of taking Arnold to his food/water area, they would take the dishes to him, placing them on the spot they wanted to use. Paul whistled and Joan bent down, letting Arnold sniff his food. She gave him a teasing taste of it and then walked him to the new chosen section. It really worked. Arnold followed, she put the dish on the floor, and Arnold hurriedly started to gulp his food down as if he had been starved for weeks. Victory on the whole front! Then Paul brought Arnold's new water dish over to him and placed it a few feet away in order not to disturb Arnold's fill-up with solid food. All was well till Arnold turned a little bit to the side and looked in the direction of his water dish. This was more than enough to incite another flight and panic reaction in the living room.

They both agreed Arnold was simply a sissy. He was obviously afraid of his own reflection in the water. They decided to make one last attempt in selecting a new dining location for him, a dark, unlit spot alongside the refrigerator. Thank heavens it worked – no more ghosts in the water dish.

All was going smoothly until Arnold's first bath. He did not mind Joan putting him in the tub. But when she started to wet him down, Arnold jumped out of the tub, took to his heels and hid in the laundry room closet.

Bathing Arnold became a major family undertaking. It took the couple's united efforts to do it. Paul would hold him in the tub and Joan would soap and rinse him. Their hope was that Arnold would get used to bathing and start to enjoy it after a while. However, the older Arnold grew, the greater his fear of being bathed. It remained a nightmare for him, and for Paul and Joan.

Arnold — Trust Overcomes Fear

Paul was getting sick and tired of the whole thing and did not want to have a sissy instead of a real dog, while Joan loved Arnold and could not imagine getting rid of him. Their marriage was also getting more and more shaky. One day, Paul strictly refused to cooperate and participate in this bathing comedy of the biggest sissy-dog he ever heard of, let alone one he owned!

As a court of last resort the veterinarian suggested some special medication for Arnold to facilitate the bathing. Instead of risking drug addiction for Arnold, the couple gave me a call. Seven weeks later I had Arnold jumping in and out of my indoor kennel pond (after removing the fish!), as a result of training based on mutual respect and trust. Three weeks later he was happily swimming with me in my big outdoor pond. Upon his return to Paul and Joan, Arnold spent the rest of the summer riding in the bow of their ski boat on Lake Berryessa.

Yes, Arnold won a true victory over water. But it was not the reflection of his own image that originally had caused his fear. It was his memory response to an incident which had happened a long, long time ago. He had fallen into the breeder's swimming pool as a seven-week-old puppy, and no one was around to rescue him immediately. When they discovered him later, he was completely exhausted and almost drowned. His front nails were worn down to the quick from his desperate and fruitless efforts to climb out of the pool that had almost become his wet grave.

The breeder had completely forgotten about this incident, and therefore not reported it to Arnold's owners. I found out by calling the breeder and asking whether any other of his dogs had ever expressed a phobia for water. Arnold had no competitors.

SUMMARY
1. Painful experiences are stored in a dog's mind and can be recalled at a later time.
2. When reprogramming a problem dog all stimuli must be excluded which are prone to trigger a negative experience from the past.
3. To give the dog a new name is an important issue because no emotions or negative experiences are connected with it, either for the owner or for the dog.

CHAPTER VI

FICTION & FACTS

"My Dog Does Not Need Training"

Let us summarize the need for training based on the cases we have studied together. The great advantage is that dogs are very trainable to fit well into our environment. Training improves the dogs' ability to process information, to learn and remember, and even to seemingly "think" and reason things out. This enables them to respond without any adverse reaction even to unknown situations. It structures and disciplines their minds in a way acceptable to our standards. Without training, they can only follow their inherited instinctive behaviors. Thus, a dog will bite a person when he feels threatened, even if this person did not intend any harm to him.

By improper training or no training, owners cripple their dogs emotionally and even physically, while believing their actions represent love, freedom, and humanity. The following story is a good illustration.

Billy—Or Love is Blind

"Good morning Mr. Meisterfeld, this is Mrs. Gordon. I hope you can give me some advice on what to do about our Billy. Something seems to be wrong with him. Billy is now three-and-a-half years old, but still whines and whimpers when I leave him, just as he did when he was a puppy. I thought he'd grow out of it, but it's gotten worse and worse.

"He just has to be with me all the time. When I go to the kitchen to prepare my husband's breakfast, within a couple of minutes Billy starts scratching at the door wanting in. When I go to the bedroom to get dressed, Billy is watching me select my dress and put on my makeup.

"I have tried to leave him at home when I went shopping, only on return to find him howling and crying. Several times he was chewing on my personal things.

"What can I do about that?"

"Sorry, Mrs. Gordon, I can't answer this question over the phone, and offer you an instant solution to your problem with Billy. I must see him and work with him in order to be able to evaluate what can be done. In addition, I would have to talk to you and your husband."

"How long would he need to stay with you? Not too long, I hope?"

When I told her about two hours, I could hear a sigh of relief. We scheduled an appointment for the next morning.

Mr. and Mrs. Gordon arrived punctually at 9:00 a.m. Mrs. Gordon got out of the car with the wiggling Billy in her arms. When she handed the little white Shih Tzu over to her husband, I could observe that all of a sudden Billy quieted down.

I explained to the couple some details about my testing procedure and asked them to come back at 11.00 a.m.

After the owners left, I observed how Billy reacted to his being kenneled for the first time in his life. He showed the normal curiosity of investigating and sniffing the inside run. Then he did the same outside and looked around. He performed a few times, then returned into his temporary living quarters and lay down.

From my observation peekhole, I could see that he remained quietly in this position for about 10 minutes. I sat down and waited. Another 10 minutes went by. Still not a whimper from Billy's run. When I looked in again, he was sound asleep. He had passed his first test of flexibility and adaptability with flying colors.

I took him out into the training ring. Billy showed no signs of any training. The sit, down, or heel commands were foreign to him. But he learned fast. After several sessions during his brief stay, he was heeling without tugging and was trying to please me. His short attention span increased from one second to several seconds.

Yes, Billy could be reprogrammed to become a well behaved, happy dog. But will he be? A detailed consultation with the owners would answer this crucial question.

The Gordons returned 15 minutes before the scheduled consultation time, giving me another clue to the emotions involved.

I explained my findings to them. When I asked them whether they had spent any time training Billy, the husband answered, "It's my wife's dog. And besides, I don't have time for that."

Then Mrs. Gordon made her statement, "I don't believe a small dog like Billy needs training. That's something only big dogs need.

Why do you think I got a small dog in the first place? In my opinion, all that's necessary is to show the pet love and kindness. I don't want to tell the dog what he should do or not do, or require him to walk on a leash. He should have his right to freedom. I don't want a four-legged tin soldier walking around the house!"

This part of the consultation is the area where some clients put up a wall of resistance and defend their position. They exaggerate their right of choice and their capacity to make the proper decisions on their own.

I have spent many hours trying to climb over this wall, only to have the client build a new one. I now use only a simple comment to this frozen-mind attitude.

"If your way worked, there would be no problem behavior in your dog. And since it does not, there might be a different, more efficient approach. Billy's behavior is the effect of his relationship with you. Without conditioning his mind through proper training, he cannot act differently than he does now."

Mr. Gordon immediately expressed his willingness to help structure Billy's mind by training him on weekends, thus giving his wife a break from her daily duties. This sounded great. Only I noticed that while he was making his offer, Mrs. Gordon was looking the other way signalling again her "no way" attitude.

I hoped that a demonstration would convince her. I brought Billy out of his run into the ring. He heeled beautifully (with a merry wagging tail) and sat and stayed.

I hoped that Mrs. Gordon could see Billy's desire and eagerness for training, thus overcoming her resistance to the idea. I pointed out that by training him, his whining, barking, and destructiveness would die out by themselves.

Mr. Gordon immediately asked whether I could give them a training program, to which I agreed. I turned Billy over to Mrs. Gordon, and we went back into the office. She sat down, holding the dog in her lap.

While I was writing a training schedule for psychological and basic obedience training needed to remedy Billy's emotional dependency, Mrs. Gordon got up and walked out of the office. She sat down on the sofa in the training hall, all the while stroking her dog (child!) heavily.

I told Mr. Gordon that his wife's attitude did not indicate a desire to change Billy's behavior, because she did not want to change her relationship with him. She, as the important link, was the reason for the dog's problem. Therefore, under these circumstances, his involvement in training Billy would be a waste of time.

I advised him to have a conversation with his wife first and come to an understanding on this issue before taking any steps. I gave him an outline for Billy's training, asking him to keep me informed of Billy's progress.

After they left, I wondered whether Mrs.Gordon really did see what was required of her. The positive change in Billy's behavior and the willingness and happiness he had expressed in the short period while I worked with him could not have escaped her attention. Since she loved the dog so dearly, what prevented her from accepting his true needs? Could her selfish love be that blind to his needs?

Do emotions block the reasoning and analytical capacities of man's mind so he can't see the truth? Unfortunately, at times it appears that way.

SUMMARY

1. An untrained problem dog is no pleasure to live with for any owner. This is one of the main reasons why every year millions of dogs are being abandoned by their owners and have to be destroyed.
2. The dogs started to cause problems owing to their environmental conditioning, i.e., improper treatment received at the hands of their owners, who did not see any need for training.
3. When a dog is left on his own to self-train, his teachers are self-gratification and survival—flight or fight. This conditions a dog to become fearful and/or aggressive.

"Train Your Dog in Five Minutes"

There is no short cut to a well-behaved dog. If a dog could be trained within a short time, we could apply this system to teaching our children.

As an intelligent species, we all know how long it takes to change an old habit, to learn something new, and to really instill it in our minds so we don't revert to the old behavior. Find out how difficult it is for you to omit only the little word "ok" from your daily conversation. Make it a habit, each time you catch yourself unconsciously saying it, to put fifty cents aside. You will have collected quite an amount as the days and weeks go by.

In one of Dr. Maltz's books on psychocybernetics he tells the story of a secretary who moved her wastebasket from the left to the right side of her desk. It took 21 days to reprogram herself to toss the waste paper to the new location rather than the old one.

How should our dogs, equipped with a lesser intelligence than ours, be able to learn new, permanent behavior patterns in a shorter time? We really expect more from a dog than we ourselves are able to accomplish even under the most favorable conditions.

It is true a dog can be taught to respond quickly to something in a certain way. One short cut to making the dog instantly obedient is the common practice of coercing the dog's will by force. This cannot insure permanent obedience, nor can it successfully be applied to all dogs, as we have already stated.

In comparison, the psychological training system, which does not claim to accomplish miracles in an unrealistic time frame, requires a certain daily routine over a period of time. At the same time, it can work with any dog, regardless of the breed, pure or mixed; regardless of sex, male, female or neutered; regardless of age or behavioral problems; from shy, stubborn and fearful to destructive, aggressive, biting, and neurotic dogs. It considers the needs of the individual dog by adjusting the amount of time for training and reprogramming, especially in the case of problem dogs. With this system the positively structured mind of a dog is not likely to become subject to a mental breakdown as is the case with a dog trained with forceful, intimidating methods.

SUMMARY

1. Permanent behavior cannot be instilled within a short time span. It takes a little bit more than five minutes to make new behavior last and create an obedient dog.
2. Intimidation techniques, used as a short cut to enforce behavior, cannot lead to permanent obedience in all dogs.
3. Only the system of psychological dog training is suitable to establish stable behavior. It can be applied successfully to all dogs without any negative consequences.

Bonding, or the Trap of Causing
Emotional Dependency and Demand

What is bonding? Bonding is the result of positive individual personal attraction leading to mutual attachment and pair and group formation. Bonding is based on common interest, is marked by exclusivity, and includes a certain amount of separation from the world outside the group.

The young puppy forms this emotional link to his mother via the pleasurable experience of feeding and being cared for. Tests carried out to reveal which factors cause a puppy to feel attracted by a human being resulted in the finding that just daily contact, without any active involvement, was enough to attain a high degree of socialization.

The dog forms his closest link with one person only over an extended period of time—his master/mistress. Other members of the family are only second choice. However, dogs do have the ability to bond with a new master if they change hands.

When behavioral problems arise in the dog, this proves that bonding is predominantly based on emotions, to the detriment of the devotional aspect. Therefore the link can easily deteriorate. Dissatisfaction results at both ends of the bond.

It is most understandable that when we have love for other living beings, be they four- or two-legged, we want the best for them. We derive great satisfaction and happiness when we can give comfort and pleasure in many forms to members of our family and friends, showing them how much we care for and love them. Yet when we extend this *human* understanding of love to our pets, and especially to our dogs, we are setting ourselves up for a baffling, emotional disappointment.

Through different "deeds" of our love and affection we attempt to "buy" (sometimes owners bargain) the love of our dogs. This can be through special cooking, offering him the place on the couch instead of limiting him to the rug, letting him sleep on our bed instead of his dog bed, giving him lots of hugs, kisses and strokes to express our affection, or hiring a sitter so he will not feel lonely when we go out to enjoy ourselves. Thus, we try to project *our* abstract thinking, ideas, and feelings about creature comfort and enjoyment on to the dog.

Hundreds of times I have been asked, "What will my dog do while I am gone all day at work? I don't want him to feel bored."

My answer is: "What do you want him to do, make the beds, do the dishes, watch TV? Why not just let him protect your home in your absence? Let me tell you a story about a dog I had to dehumanize."

Ronny

Sue was very happy with her Great Dane puppy, Ronny, and the love and affection he expressed for her. She cuddled, stroked, and hugged him a lot, following the information she had read about the importance of bonding with the puppy at an early age, and that it can be intensified with lots of physical contact, such as hugging, kissing, picking the dog up and carrying him around. Sue, a true believer, followed this advice with Ronny as often as she could. Sue told me Ronny would lie on the couch with his head in her lap watching TV with her for hours. It seemed that the dog actually did view the programs. Ronny kept her feet warm by sleeping at the foot of the bed. (This was one of the reasons Sue had acquired a shorthaired dog.) Ronny loved to jog with Sue, and this was very easy for him, with his long legs. Ronny was very friendly to everybody, even to Sue's male clients and occasional weekend guests.

Sue's happiness was complete. She had a faithful companion who thrived on affection and returned it, who enjoyed the same things in life as she did, like TV soap operas and jogging. Plus he did not mind if she worked long hours in her business, which she operated out of her home. There was no need to negotiate "What should we have for dinner today?" or "Let's watch a different program!" There was never any reason for controversy, as it used to be with her ex-husband all the time. Sue was convinced her pet was the best deal she had ever made. A dream had come true, she had found the ideal partner for life.

If Sue had to leave the house and could not possibly take Ronny with her, a dog sitter would come over to keep the pet from getting lonely and bored. Sue could not live with the guilt feeling of forcing Ronny to go on a howling, moaning spree like "The Hound of the Baskervilles."

One time Sue had to be away from home for a couple of hours and could not take Ronny with her. Unfortunately, the sitter was not available and the neighbor did not have the spare time to keep Ronny company. Sue turned on the radio to drown out Ronny's howling blues, and hurried to finish her business. When she returned home,

Ronny had expressed and manifested his "I missed you terribly." Not only had he been moaning the blues and chewing up Sue's bedspread, he also had had a spell of diarrhea in the bedroom. Sue never repeated this mistake. From then on she was faithful to Ronny. For the next two years they were always together, an inseparable pair.

One day Sue forgot her briefcase in her car. Ronny was sound asleep. So Sue quietly stepped out of the apartment door and rushed to the carport. The moment she reached her car, there was a loud smashing sound of breaking glass. Sue turned around abruptly, just in time to witness Ronny flying through her second-story bedroom window in a desperate attempt to remain at her side.

Miraculously, Ronny survived. No fractured bones, with only minor cuts from the broken window glass. The veterinarian who sutured the wounds suggested that Sue should seek some advice, and that there was a flaw in their relationship. Ronny was, without doubt, humanized.

After ten weeks of dehumanizing therapy for Ronny's emotional dependency, Sue was able to leave him alone without even a baby sitter. Ronny was pleased in his new role of protecting his mistress' property. He greeted her always with a wagging tail when she returned. Now they were both truly happy and content, a perfect match.

Usually, loving and affectionate dog owners expect the same in return from their pet. They are very disappointed when they don't get it and when the dog becomes demanding and reacts with jealousy, possessiveness, destructiveness, and other adverse behaviors culminating in biting instead. The problem is, we forget that a dog is a *dog* and not a human being with different perceptions and means of self-expression. When a dog feels in danger (real danger or just an unknown situation he cannot cope with), he will bite as a natural reaction of self-defense.

By using his dog as a human substitute, object of worship and emotional satisfaction, the well-meaning dog owner overwhelms and frustrates his pet tremendously. The dog gets trapped in a kind of limbo world. He tries, but is unable to perform like a human being, and loses in some instances even the drive to identify or relate with his own kind. He becomes hostile towards other dogs, refuses to breed or to be bred, etc.

The repercussions of this negative development are even more far-reaching. According to my decades of experience with problem dogs, the breeding of emotionally conditioned dogs can produce a new breed type. Thanks to the puppy mills, this new breed is already flourishing and multiplying. Water-shy retrievers without the desire to retrieve and bird dogs uninterested in hunting are distinct examples.

Is this the result of human arrogance or lack of knowledge? I see the main reasons as misunderstanding of dog behavior and misconceptions about the special responsibilities involved in owning a dog. In my opinion, the most detrimental factors in human/canine relationships are:

1. Equality—When the owner sees the dog as "one of the family."
   a. The dog *has* the same rights as humans.
   b. The dog *demands* the same rights as humans.
2. Humanization and catering
   a. The dog is permanently pampered, coddled, and catered to.
   b. The dog is not treated as an animal, but as a person which is contradictory to the laws of nature.
3. Double standards, inconsistency, and impatience are combined with unclear, incomprehensive, communication and negative training techniques.
4. The dog is not trained at all by the owner and has to self-train.

The dog cannot handle this role. Instead of developing devotion, his emotions become wrongly conditioned. When his emotional and other demands are not being met, he responds with aggression and destruction, and he develops phobias.

SUMMARY

1. A humanized, self-trained dog becomes either emotionally dependent—flipping out when left alone, or emotionally demanding—barking and howling excessively, demanding his owner stay with him at all times.
2. An emotionally dependent dog's willingness to please becomes a demand to be pleased instead. He never seems to be satisfied.
3. The bonding between master and dog can only remain firm when its foundations are understanding, acceptance, consideration, communication, respect, and trust.
4. Such a bond can only be established through psychological training.

Schizophrenic Dogs, or the Conditioning
of Dr. Jekyll and Mr. Hyde

Dogs who suddenly change personalities from friendly to aggressive and back to friendly again are generally labeled schizophrenic and considered unsalvageable. This behavior anomaly is usually ascribed to their genes.

I will not deny the existence of schizophrenia in dogs. I also agree with the general opinion of dog authorities that these dogs cannot be changed with the widely practiced training methods based on negative reinforcement. However, according to my long experience with dogs showing the symptoms of schizophrenia, the reasons for this kind of behavior can predominantly be traced back to the environmental conditioning that developed it. It was always a "love/hate" relationship on both sides.

It is indirectly true that the behavioral responses of these dogs originated in their genes:

1. With the negative conditioning they had sustained, their survival instinct was permanently triggered. They could not help responding to threats with what can be termed a critical reaction.
2. Their ranking order instinct was involved.

All these "schizo dogs" had three common denominators:

1. They were conditioned with forceful methods, i.e., with pain and punishment.
2. The dogs were very intelligent, sensitive, and had a high will-to-power.
3. Their owners were not their masters, but attempted to dominate the dogs occasionally. This was interrupted by periods of extensive permissiveness and affection so that their interactions with their dogs were based on inconsistency and confusion.

In many cases the problem was aggravated if the owner instantly shifted from punishment to affection. A dog is deeply confused when he is punished or reprimanded for a mistake and immediately afterwards is praised and showered with "vigorous" affection. However, some famous trainers recommend this, reasoning that it is necessary to prove to the dog that you still love him even after his wrongdoing and your reprimand. The problem with this concept is that a dog's

DR. JEKYLL AND MR. HYDE

mind cannot reason abstractly and is not capable of overriding the fear experience of punishment with being instantly showered with hugs and praise. Even with developed human minds it takes several minutes (in some people as much as hours and days, in others forever) for the emotions of fear and anger to subside, before they are truly receptive to the opposite experience of praise and affection.

The dog tolerates this confusing behavior until his will-to-power is strong enough, or until his tolerance threshold is reached. The increasing frustration and aggression accumulates in the dog's memory bank until it is discharged on an outlet-serving object. The dog then reacts with his inborn defense mechanism by exhibiting disobedience growing to violence. This is sometimes triggered by events or situations not obvious to the owner. It is directed against objects, animals, people, especially children whom the dog identifies as subordinates, and even against the owner himself. At one moment the dog is very friendly, and then, without any obvious reason or forewarning, in the next instant suddenly flips into opposite, violent behavior due to a mental and adrenal overload.

The basic problem is that humans, in contrast to dogs, are able to sort out mixed messages, even double standards in social relations. We learn early in life to read between the lines. We play different roles according to what we perceive is necessary in order to project a favorable image of ourselves to gain recognition or reward. We have an acceptable behavior in public, and a different one (the real me) when we are in the safe boundaries of our home environment. This is our typical way of life and interrelating.

Unfortunately, we expect man's best friend also to have these capabilities. Although dogs have a limited reasoning capacity, they lack the complex rationality of the human mind and are incapable of understanding our widely practiced double standards. When a dog is permitted to sit on the sofa today and tomorrow this is prohibited, he will be at a loss to understand and will become confused. He also will lose respect and trust for his owner. The same applies when the owner permits the dog to disobey commands today and punishes him tomorrow for this disobedience.

When a dog is trained with such contradictions, and experiences that the virtue of today is the punished crime of tomorrow, he inevitably develops mixed feelings and a split personality—a Dr. Jekyll and Mr. Hyde.

By getting to the cause of this abnormal, schizophrenic behavior, and using positive psychological methods in re-training, I have been able to successfully rehabilitate such dogs without any drugs or punishment. The owners changed their attitudes toward their dogs, ensuring maintenance of "normal" behavior without fear of their dog reverting. The magic formula for this was to establish an atmosphere of clear communication based on mutual respect, trust, and reliability right from the start.

These dogs never again exhibited schizophrenic symptoms. They became reliable, well-balanced pets instead.

SUMMARY

1. All so-called "schizo" dogs I have evaluated and reprogrammed started off in the family as normal, friendly, and affectionate puppies.
2. Due to their environmental conditioning they became "schizophrenic" and expressed this behavior only later in life; some of them at the age of seven to twelve months, others when they were two or three years old, or even older.
3. These dogs could be reprogrammed with psychological methods and remained normal with their enlightened owners.

"My Dog Reacts Aggressively Toward Children — They Must Have Abused Him"

Some examples prove that a dog can be afraid of children due to former abuse by them. However, in the majority of incidents when a dog attacks children, other reasons are involved. According to my experience, in many cases the dog did not even have prior contact with children.

By forming mental pictures of the objects around them and by incorporating this information into their memory banks, dogs store details about the appearance of persons they are familiar with. When they are only around adults and suddenly encounter a child less than half an adult's size, this realization triggers dominant behavior. This behavior can be expressed, if a dog has not been trained or has been trained using negative methods. The problem then is that the dog regards children as inferiors. This makes them more susceptible to attack. It does not even matter whether he has encountered children before or not.

When you train your dog with force, punishment, and the "glaring magic of your eyes," you just suppress his will-to-power toward you. At the same time, you are conditioning him to express it toward a lower level. This can mean aggressive behavior toward a woman, or especially toward children, who are smaller and physically weaker.

Unfortunately, many untrained dogs who grew up with children and were not abused by them at all turned violently against them. Romeo was one of these dogs.

Romeo, or Confusion

Romeo was a cuddly and fluffy little puppy sitting in his mistress' lap while she was watching TV. He was having a little difficulty trying to understand why his master, upon returning from a four-day absence didn't share his wife's enthusiasm for him. On the contrary, his master had a "don't touch" attitude. When Romeo tried to be affectionate with his master, he often got smacked. Then, when the master would take off on another trip, he would jump back in the lap of his mistress, where he received constant caressing. This was his programming. I call it "hot and cold," from one extreme to the other.

There were happy times, though, when Romeo slept in his master's bed, while he was gone. The day arrived when a change in at least one of Romeo's habits became imperative. With Romeo weighing in at 110 pounds and his mistress at 102, it got to the point that once he was on her lap, there was no getting him off. She could not convince him that it wasn't cute anymore, and he should now remain on the floor. She could not accomplish this sudden change, but the next time her husband returned Romeo got a severe whipping. After that he stayed on the floor. Now his mistress would get down with him on the floor and cuddle and pet him there. Only now he did not respond as happily as before. He just seemed to tolerate it.

One day, when Romeo was 20 months old, a neighbor came over with her little daughter who had been playing with him since he was a pup. However, this time, when she was giving the 150-pound fluff hugs and kisses, he nipped her. Automatically, the incident was regarded as the child's fault. She must have hurt him. (She was five years old.) So the neighbor made sure that her daughter did not visit

Romeo anymore.

About six months later a boy of 12 was petting Romeo, and the master was watching the relationship, which was seemingly enjoyable for both. Suddenly, without warning, Romeo bit the boy. The owner then arrived at the conclusion that the dog did not like children, basically because he was not raised with any. (Yet the little girl was part of his puppyhood.) A new fear crept into the owners' minds, that Romeo could seriously harm a child. So children were not permitted to make contact with him anymore. Problem solved!

Then one day an adult friend, while petting him, did not hear the rumble in Romeo's throat. After a few minutes the dog bit him.

At this point I was called. They had been advised by their veterinarian to put the dog to sleep. Yes, I said, this would certainly take care of the biting problem, but there was a chance that Romeo's lifespan could be extended beyond his present two years without biting. So Romeo was brought to me for evaluation and consultation. We found that the reason for the dog's problem was emotional, which in turn developed into lack of respect and low tolerance.

During our conversation, the owner's wife's emotional needs for contact and affection were brought to the surface, which, in a servile way, were met by Romeo. However, the dog had to carry a heavy emotional burden from the mistress, and at the same time had to relate to his master's completely cold and hostile attitude. Romeo had to serve two camps, which was far beyond his capabilities.

Romeo was reprogrammed as a working dog, and the couple had training sessions, in which their emotional relationship with the dog was desensitized. A new and balanced man-woman-dog relationship was then developed. Of course, this required a re-evaluation of the couple's relationship with each other. The husband, formerly a workaholic, now became aware of his wife's deeper inner needs.

This story shows how sometimes the solution to a distressing "dog problem" can be a happy one not only for the dog but for the owners as well.

SUMMARY

1. It is a wrong general assumption that a dog expresses hostile behavior toward children because he was abused by them.
2. When a dog was not trained or was trained with dominant, forceful methods, he regards children as inferiors and below

himself in the pecking order.
3. He will express his position with aggressive behavior.

"Give Your Dog Lots of Hugs and Kisses"— VERY DANGEROUS ADVICE

Not only the books on dogs but also the media, with TV programs, commercials and advertisements are full of scenes indicating that it is very desirable to have close facial contact with a dog to express love and affection. "Shower him with hugs and kisses" is one of the many slogans. Another one, recommended by a trainer, is "Put butter on your nose to encourage his kissing".

Beyond the hygienic problem of possibly contracting diseases from the dog, the greatest danger in this respect is a facial bite. Again, there is a strong natural instinct for the dog to bite, not only to defend himself when he feels attacked, but also to express dominance over his own kind and other species. When dogs compete in this respect and get into a serious or playful fight, they prefer to bite each other around the face and head. They practice this behavior from early puppyhood and during their whole adult life. The same behavior can be triggered when you put your face near a dog's head showing your teeth. The dog can perceive this as a threat or power play and bite you in the face.

The other side of the coin is that a submissive dog tries to lick the face of the dominant one in order to show his servitude to his superior. However, when you (as his "master" and authority figure) initiate this behavior by approaching the dog and kissing him, you seriously confuse your pet. By doing this you imitate the behavior of a subordinate dog. On the other hand, you demand obedience from him as his master. Your dog really does not know who is who in this relationship and has therefore to find out through power play and challenge.

The danger is increased when the dog is not trained or is trained with wrong methods, such as the dominance/alpha wolf method, which strongly conditions this behavior.

Children are especially at risk. The head of a small child crawling on the floor, or even when erect, is on the same level or beneath the dog's head. When a child plays with the dog, the dog can perceive this as a challenge and bite the child's face. (See picture, Page 83)

This is supported by the following article:

"Dog Bites and Children's Faces"

(Excerpted from the 11/84 issue of The Harvard Medical School Health Letter, ©1984, President and Fellows of Harvard College)

"A relatively serious and unsolved public health problem is the high frequency with which dogs bite the faces of people, especially children. If results from a careful study conducted in Wisconsin hold true for the United States as a whole, there are some 44,000 *facial* injuries a year from dog bites, and of these 16,000 are severe. Almost all of the worst, and potentially disfiguring, injuries affect children under the age of 10. Treatment is made especially difficult by the fact that dog bites tend to tear delicate facial structures, such as eyelids and lips. Although very little is known about the circumstance that lead to biting, some educated guesses can be made. *Most bites appear to be inflicted by pets in familiar surroundings, and fewer than 6% are brought on by teasing or abuse.* Many dogs normally bite each other around the head and mouth as part of aggressive play, and it may be that such dogs approach children in the same spirit, not reacting defensively and not 'intending' to injure their victims. An innocent gesture of the child's may simply be misinterpreted by the dog as an invitation to bite.

"The most obvious protective measures—reminding children to keep their faces away from dogs and keeping close watch on toddlers—are probably also the least effective, as Trudy Karlson, the author of the Wisconsin study, observes. More stringent leash laws are also generally beside the point, *as half of all facial bites to children under 4 are inflicted by their own pets, and 90% of the children in this age group are bitten while at home.*

"Probably the most useful step would be for families with young children to avoid keeping large, aggressive dogs as household pets. Unfortunately, little is known as to which breeds are apt to engage in facial biting. Some evidence indicates that working and sporting breeds pose the greatest risk, as do young dogs (males more than females). German shepherds, malamutes, and huskies seem to be high-risk breeds, whereas hounds may have less inclination to bite than other breeds. Regardless of breed, dogs should never be left alone with a small child, even when the child seems to be protected by a playpen or crib." *(Journal of the AMA, June 22/29, 1984).*

In reality, the frequency of facial bites is much much greater than 44,000, as hundreds of thousands of facial bites are not reported.

At almost every contact I learn from dog owners that some member of the immediate family, relatives or friends sustained a facial dog bite, often labeled a nip, at one time or another in their lives. For this reason, I strongly recommend abstaining from any facial contact with a dog of any breed, even the family pet, because of the possibility for a misunderstanding on the dog's part and the safety hazards involved. Remember, young children mimic the behavior of adults. And even though it may be safe for you to kiss your dog and it is accepted by him, it may not be an accepted contact when attempted by your child or grandchild.

The dog will be highly satisfied and happy when he gets pats on the chest and shoulder area. Many dogs don't even like to be hugged. They openly show their aversion by whining and howling and trying to escape from what they perceive to be a restraint.

We have to comprehend that dogs have a different understanding with regard to receiving affection. They need to deserve it, and affection should be given to them in a way which they cannot misinterpret.

SUMMARY
1. Remember, your dog has been practicing facial biting since puppyhood. This behavior is accepted and expected among all dogs as a natural behavior pattern.
2. Therefore, without proper, respectful training your dog is not aware that this behavior is not tolerable with human beings.
3. Young children, who are the most frequent victims of facial dog bites, have to be protected. They should never be left alone with a dog.
4. *Because children mimic adult behavior,* adults should not demonstrate facial contact with a dog in their presence!

Pups Practicing Aggression

Play-Agressive Head and Face Biting

CHAPTER VII
HIGHLIGHTS — THE BETTER WAY

When Your Dog is Disobedient

If your dog refuses to follow a command, you should find the cause for his disobedience rather than going into punishment-by-force correction.

Have you taken the time to educate your dog's mind, and have you used respectful training methods? Is it possible the dog misunderstood you, is fearful and mistrusts you so much that he is not willing to endanger himself with something, which his discriminating mind has not recorded as a friendly situation, person, or object? You cannot expect trust from your dog if you punish him and make him fearful of you. As a consequence, every time you approach your dog, he feels insecure. He does not know if he will he praised or punished.

What is the most deep-rooted instinct in an animal's mind? Survival. So when you have him on this level, he is not too concerned about pleasing you or responding to your commands due to his fear. With a high-will-to power like Doc/Jellybean, he may not even wait until you come close to him. He actually goes after you rather than waiting for the contact which he anticipates as punishment and pain, based on his experience.

Then ask yourself, are you the dog's master or is he yours? If he is the master, then of course he does not see any need to obey you if it does not suit him. Your correction will not change his position, if you don't change yours.

There are dogs who show a lot of adrenal conditioning and are heavily charged up, especially when they are used to running wild in the field, chasing other animals, cars, bicycles, joggers and even children. They get hyper and excited about all the things they encounter.

This type of dog should not be reprogrammed in a class environment with other dogs and people around. What Jellybean and many other dogs I have worked with need is one-to-one concentration, so the handler is the only main stimulus. When there are too many stimuli around, the dog gets distracted, and it is not possible to strengthen and discipline his mind. He cannot learn to focus his attention completely on the necessary programming. The conditioning will take forever and will never be very solid.

I highly recommend working with your problem dog on a one-to-one basis without as few distractions as possible. You and the dog will be distracted by spectators, even family members. Even if your only concern is your performance level, it will be sufficient to shorten and split your attention span. With his exceptional perception and discrimination, the dog will immediately notice that you are distracted and not pay the necessary attention to you. This will slow the process of disciplining his mind and controlling his responses as well as establishing trust in you. You will have to correct the dog to overcome his incorrect responses, and this increases his fear and mistrust. In this stage of training the dog should not be reprimanded at all.

You need a dog's trust to make him perform willingly and voluntarily. *There is no command to make a person or dog respect and trust you; and you cannot "punish" trust and respect into a dog.* The better options you have to reach this goal are:

- Show him respect and trust.
- Teach him to respect and trust you by handling him only in a positive way. Then a dog is more than willing to work with you, because respect and trust are the preconditions for the manifestation of servitude.

Nobody gets servitude from his dog by merely walking him around everyday for a few hours and making him heel, sit, and stay. These commands are just the necessary mechanics. *It is your overall attitude, your state of mind and emotions* that the dog is picking up and processing in his mind. Therefore, this is the point to start.

In my workshops and individually working with clients and their problem dogs, I require *them* to reprogram themselves. In many cases, their attitudes and concepts need to be modified, and sometimes completely changed. This involves some of their emotional needs.

What will happen if they don't get in touch with their subconscious responses, their thoughts, feelings and emotions, before the dog returns to his home after reprogramming? The dog will revert. This is really less a reversion than a habitual response to a relationship and behavior pattern the owner originally conditioned.

There is one book I consider very useful to all owners of problem dogs and always recommend, and even ask them to read, *"As Man*

Thinketh", by James Allen. The bottom line is that the owner must firmly believe the reprogramming will be successful, and then it will.

SUMMARY

1. Don't force your dog with punishment to obey when he dos not follow your commands.
2. Rather than angrily reacting to his refusal to obey, analyze the cause for it.
3. By eliminating the reason for your dog's disobedience you gain his obedience.
4. Before you start reprogramming your dog, focus on yourself first and *start your own reprogramming.* You cannot teach what you haven't learned; you cannot give what you don't have.
5. If you are constantly waiting for an opportunity to punish your dog, you are angry with someone else, and you project this onto the dog. When the dog does something wrong, you feel justified in expressing this anger toward the dog.
6. It is very important to get in touch with your own mental and emotional state prior to handling your dog.
7. If you keep doing the same things, the same things will keep happening!

The Art of Using Praise and Correction in a Healthy Way

Dogs thrive on praise for good performance. Verbal correction is usually sufficient to make a dog aware of wrongdoing. As mentioned before, praise immediately following a correction confuses a dog. The dog is at a loss to understand what is going on. He did something wrong for which he is being corrected, either verbally or physically. At the same time the handler lets the dog know, through his praise, that he did something good. Did he do something right or wrong? Well, it must have been something right, or why the reward? If this method is applied on a large scale, and depending on the dog's sensitivity, his confusion can grow to paranoia (See Schizophrenic Dogs).

How would you feel, if someone yelled at you, slapped you in the face, and immediately afterward overwhelmed you with praise and hugs. Even children brought up in this way cannot establish any trust in their parents, becoming totally insecure and confused. Sometimes correction is essential. When necessary, it should never be done in an emotional manner, but matter-of-factly. When you discipline your misbehaving dog, don't be angry, don't shout at him or hit him. This usually aggravates the problem. Instead use a simple oral correction, such as the word "Nein" (HOWS & WHYS...) immediately when the undesired behavior is manifesting.

A reprimand done some time after the undesired event will usually not be very effective. Under normal circumstances the dog will refer it to what he is doing at that moment. When you correct him while he is lying down, you teach him not to lie down. When you reprimand him while he is approaching you, you condition him to stay away from you. Don't correct your dog too often. This conditions him in a more negative direction. Rather, concentrate on positive reinforcement to encourage good behavior by showing and telling the dog what he should do. When he follows your commands obediently, then praise is very appropriate and supports and instills this new behavior. This helps to bury the remains of undesired behavior.

Don't use *heavy stroking* as a reward. It will stimulate his emotional reactions and thus his adrenals. Instead, use *pats,* which convey praise without the negative side effect of exciting the dog. To ensure a positive performance in your dog and to minimize the necessity of correction, the use of the Unity-Praise-Principle (HOWS & WHYS...) is highly recommended, because it is a proven method for permanently implanting the new positive behavior in your dog.

SUMMARY

1. Correct your dog without putting out negative feelings.
2. Always perform the correction immediately when the negative behavior occurs.
3. Correct as little as possible; a simple verbal correction should be adequate.
4. Show your dog the right behavior.
5. Let your dog earn his praise. Praise him only if he follows your commands, but don't overdo it. Praise after every third or fourth correct response is sufficient.
6. Praise should be short, simple, sincere—without gushing or overemotion.
7. Use the Unity-Praise-Principle to reinforce obedience to the commands.

The Primary Needs of a Dog Within the Family Structure

1. The clear definition of his position from the beginning with all the consequences involved for each family member.
2. Meeting the dog's needs. The dog is dependent on his owner(s) to ensure his well-being by fulfilling his basic needs:
   a. Physical needs:
      - to feed him properly
      - to take care of his health
   b. Emotional needs:
      - to give him a sense of security by having the owner assume the position of master under any and all circumstances;
      - to always be consistent in your interrelation with him;
      - to ensure his feeling of importance and satisfaction by giving him the opportunity to repay his owner by serving and pleasing;
      - to reward him for his devotion with love and appropriate affection.
   c. Psychological needs:
      - to establish with your dog a system of communication with consistent commands and words, which he can understand;
      - to teach him consistent behavioral standards to enable him to optimally cope with his environment;
      - to effect his training in a pleasant and efficient way based on the concepts of mutual respect and trust.

The Ideal Master/Dog Relationship

1. The owner trains his dog from an early age with psychological methods.
2. The owner establishes territorial and psychological boundaries for the dog.
3. Consistency, clear communication, respect, and trust are the foundations for the dog's feeling of security.

A Personal Experience
at the Sonoma County Humane Society Shelter

There has been a good deal of controversy regarding our Humane Society here in Sonoma County, California, which may be typical of a national problem. For those who feel it's cruel to destroy an innocent puppy or kitten... I agree! Yet I would highly recommend to individuals who think our HS personnel are cold and callous that they volunteer a day or two a week to better find out what is really happening behind the front office. Did I say volunteer... yes! Because volunteers are the ones doing the feeding, cleaning and other necessary chores.

I had the pleasure of meeting one of these people behind the cyclone fencing. Her name was Dee. After I was given permission by a very cooperative Wes Draper, the executive director, to photograph some puppies, I could observe that Dee expressed nothing but love and affection for the pups. She knew full well that after the morning feeding the office manager might find it necessary to "put down" some of the affectionate and friendly pups. Why? Because of *input-output!* When more stray homeless dogs are arriving than being adopted and there is no more space, there is only one option left. I accidentally witnessed it.

On my first visit, I saw four puppies in a run that looked ideally suited for the pictures I needed. They were friendly and responsive, but because it was too hot that day, their performance was not high. I made arrangements to return at a later date and, because of previous commitments, I had to wait two days.

When I returned...lo and behold, three of the four were gone. I remembered Dee telling me that they had overstayed their clearance time for adoption, yet because they were so nice, they had been held over. Even though I wished they were present, I was happy someone appreciated them and had given them a home.

Because Dee was busy feeding, I had requested permission to look around and find some others. As I traveled down run after run I was amazed at the variety of homeless dogs, from puppies to full-grown, standing at their kennel gates and wagging their tails. I decided to revisit a beautifully marked German Shepherd in the end run. I figured the previous owner must have spent a lot of time training him.

The Shepherd had obediently responded to a few commands the first time I saw him. He was gone. I felt good, because I assumed he too had found a home. As I walked by the end door in order to reach another section of runs, I passed by a small room to my left. With no one watching, I took a peek through the window.

There was the German Shepherd, lying on a stainless steel table with one of the Yellow Lab puppies alongside him. Sadly, they had both arrived at their last destination. The scene was similar to a freeze frame on my VCR—not moving.

As a dog breeder, I was once sitting on the fence regarding what the Humane Society of Sonoma County (and other counties) has been trying to say to pet owners..."You *can* make a difference. Spaying and neutering is the only answer." I now agree that this is the best choice for dog owners who are not planning on a selective breeding program. Here are some suggestions recommended by the Humane Society that can be applied in any state regarding our pets. The advice is good and sound.

Spaying or Neutering Your Pet

Communities which support and practice pet population control have fewer animal problems, fewer lists of "throwaway pets" lining their daily newspaper columns, and fewer animals being euthanized at pounds and shelters.

Keeping Your Pet Licensed, Leashed and Under Your Supervision

Free roaming pets bite, destroy property, cause accidents, breed randomly, and soil the streets. Remember, your neighbor may not love your pet as much as you do—he may have good reason not to.

Being a Responsible Pet Owner

By being a responsible pet owner and properly caring for your pet, you are setting a good example for others to follow.

By providing your pet with shelter, food and veterinary care, as well as giving him attention and affection, you demonstrate your commitment to kindness.

YES, MAN'S BEST FRIEND NEEDS HELP! I hope, with this new understanding of his behavior, YOU WILL BE ABLE TO PROVIDE IT.

C.W. Meister

Canine Companions for Independence
P.O. Box 446 · Santa Rosa, CA 95402

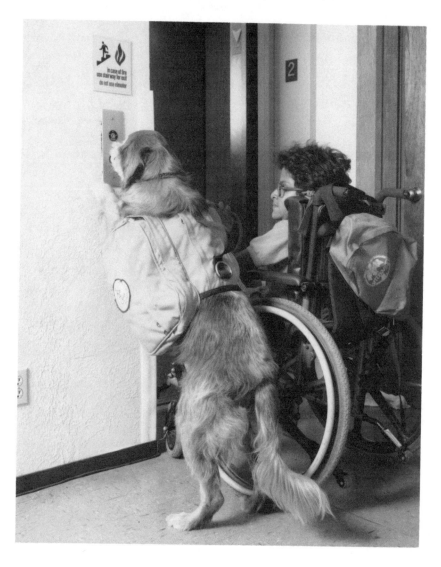

Canine Companions for Independence
Service Dog, Ivy, Pushes an Elevator Button for Her Master.

Examples of the Dog's Unique Willingness to Please Us.

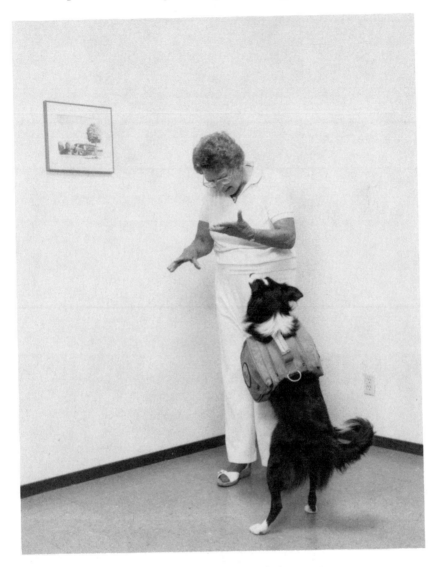

Canine Companions for Independence
Signal Dog, Jane, Alerts Her Mistress to an Important Sound.

Canine Companions for Independence
Social Dog Can Add Vitality and Purpose
for Those Who Need it Most.

Canine Companions for Independence
Service Dog, Joker, and His Master Team Up
to Overcome Another Barrier.

BIBLIOGRAPHY

Griffin D.R., "*Animal Thinking*," Cambridge and London: Harvard University Press, 1963

Humphrey E. and Warner L., "*Working Dogs*," Baltimore: The Johns Hopkins Press, 1934

Lorenz K., "*On Aggression*," New York: Bantam Books, Inc., 1977

Sokolov, Y.N., "*Perception and the Conditioned Reflex*," Oxford, London, New York, Paris: Pergamon Press, 1963

BYE-EE!

SERVICES AND PRODUCTS AVAILABLE

1. C.W. Meisterfeld, a member of the National Speakers Association, gives **PRESENTATIONS** on the different aspects of dog behavior and canine/human relationships. Topics include:

   - Dog/Human Behavior Parallels
   - Does Fido Run Your Life?
   - Understand What Your Dog Is Trying To Tell You

2. **Full Day or evening SEMINARS** on:
   - Canine Behavior & Psychological Dog Training

3. Audio **CASSETTE ALBUMS:**
   - *Canine Behavioral Psychology*
   - *Psychological Dog Training*

4. **VHS VIDEOS:**
   - *A Safe & Humane Approach to Dog Behavior* (Educational)
   - *Canine Capers* (Humorous, with costume
     dog "Sir Walter")
   - *Mutual Respect Behavior Management*
     Comprehensive, dramatic analysis of true life, in-house management behavior. Valuable, practical principles to improve efficiency, productivity and morale.

For additional information please contact:

MEISTERFELD & ASSOCIATES
448 Seavey, Suite 9
Petaluma, CA 94952
Tel. (707) 763-0056

###

To order a copy of **JELLYBEAN,** please see next page.

BOOKS

- For one copy of **JELLYBEAN** ($19.95), please add $4.50 for postage & handling.

- For 2 copies, we pay the postage.

- For 3-4 copies, we pay the postage plus 10% discount.

- For larger orders/discounts, please contact us.

  (California residents, please add sales tax)

Other books by C.W. Meisterfeld:

- *Tails of a Dog Psychoanalyst*
- *Hows & Whys of Psychological Dog Training*

  Please note *Hows & Whys* is out of print and is replaced with the updated book titled
- *Psychological Dog Training*

M R K PUBLISHING
448 Seavey, Suite 9
Petaluma, CA 94952
(707) 763-0056